Garden for Life

University Extension Press
Extension Division, University of Saskatchewan

Dean of the Extension Division: Gordon Thompson
Managing Editor of the Press: Bertram Wolfe
Associate Editor: Roberta Mitchell Coulter
Coordinator of Agricultural/Horticultural Publications: Bruce Hobin

For this Publication

Editors: Geri Rowlatt, Sara Williams, Bert Wolfe, Stan Rooker, Roberta Mitchell Coulter
Technical Advisor: Sara Williams

Garden for Life

Horticulture for People with Special Needs

Lynn Dennis

University Extension Press

Extension Division, University of Saskatchewan

Cover photograph of *(l to r)* Vern Friebel, Christine Wiercinski, and Kathy Wiebe by Bert Wolfe. Cover design by Roberta Coulter.

Printed in Canada
02 01 00 99 98 97 96 95 94   5 4 3 2 1

In addition to those noted with individual excerpts, the following publishers have generously given permission to use extended quotations from copyrighted works.
    The excerpt on page 2 copyright 1988 Time Inc. Reprinted by permission.
    Table 4 from an article by Rosalyn Dodd in Growth Point, HT No. 125, Horticultural Therapy, Goulds Ground, Vallis Way, Frome, Somerset, BA11 3DW.

Canadian Cataloguing in Publication Data

Dennis, Lynn

    Garden for life

    Includes bibliographical references.
    ISBN 0–88880–313–3

1. Gardening - Therapeutic use. I. Title.

RM735.7.G37D4 1994   615'.8515   C94–920221–5

Contents

➤─┤─◆➤─○─◆─┤─◄

Chapter 1
"Life Began in a Garden"   1

Figures

⊰─┤◆►─◆─○─◄◆─├─≺

Tables

⊱──•◦•──⊰

Foreword

⊱—⬦⊶◦⊷⬦—⊰

Garden for Life is compulsory reading for all those interested in the use of horticulture as therapy. We are most fortunate to have Lynn Dennis, an enthusiast, who over twenty years has had the opportunity not only to practice Horticultural Therapy at the highest level, but also to pass on his vast knowledge of the subject to others by arranging seminar and study days.

This very well researched teaching manual covers a wide range of subjects relating to this fairly new discipline by suggesting activities for all ages from the very young to those of us approaching the final stages of life. His experience, which he shares with his readers, is extensive and will be an inspiration to all who wish to be involved in this very worthwhile activity. His advice will help not only beginners, but also those readers already actively involved in Horticultural Therapy.

The author carefully explains how to go about starting up a project. The detailed charts go as far as stating exact sums required to purchase essential equipment.

Ways to help the less able to continue to enjoy their hobby by altering garden layouts and adapting tools are clearly explained and fully illustrated. There are suggestions to increase the involvement of passive gardeners by arranging visits to local parks to collect materials for crafts, opening up a whole new area of interest in the subject. Bird watching and photography are also included in those visits.

In his book Lynn Dennis deals very adequately with all aspects of Horticultural Therapy in an easy-to-read style. I commend it to all with any interest in this form of gardening.

Andrew Sinclair White
Research Officer, National Health Service (retired)
Associate of Honour, Royal Horticultural Society
Churchill Fellow 1975

Acknowledgements

>─┼─◆>─◆─○─◆┤─◆┤─<

I am grateful to the many people who through the years have provided the inspiration and encouragement essential to completing this project.

Special thanks are extended to Hazel Clarkson, Department of Physical Therapy, University of Alberta, and Lorraine Dahlberg, Occupational Therapy Consultant, Edmonton, for the valuable contribution and insight into developing the text. Special thanks are also extended to the Alberta Teachers' Association Educational Trust and the Canadian Occupational Therapists' Association for their generous support.

My compliments and sincere appreciation are extended to Melanie Eastley for the illustrations, and to Lu Ziola for her help in producing the manuscript.

Finally, to my wife, Valerie, whose encouragement and support helped make the project possible, I am most grateful.

Introduction

For centuries people have been aware of the healing power of gardens. In recent years this awareness has grown and horticulture is being recognized more and more as a valuable therapy at hospitals, nursing homes, and other health care settings.

Garden for Life introduces this aspect of horticulture to caregivers. Horticulture therapy is the application of horticultural practices and principles in a therapeutic setting to improve the physical, emotional, social, and/or spiritual state of your clients.

Horticulture is an excellent path to this goal for many reasons. Gardening demonstrates the value of caring, patience, and persistence. It produces tangible rewards, like beautiful flowers and delicious vegetables. In a garden, one is constantly aware of and stimulated by changes in the seasons, the life cycles of plants and insects, changing weather patterns — by all the miracles of nature. A garden can provide a relaxed, nonthreatening place to meet and talk with friends. A garden is filled with analogies for human life, analogies that can help your clients grow toward greater awareness and understanding of themselves and others.

For horticulture therapy to be effective, gardens and gardening must be enjoyable for your clients. This book describes methods to make gardening easier and more pleasurable for people with special needs, including the institutionalized, physically challenged, seniors, children, the visually impaired, or those who are emotionally disturbed. Although the book is designed to be a manual for professionals and volunteers who wish to use horticulture therapy with their clients, it also has gardening ideas that all gardeners will find useful.

Blending gardening and horticulture science with the therapeutic aspects of life and well-being is the focus of *Garden for Life*, and while the book describes techniques for using horticulture and gardens in therapy, the therapist is expected to use his or her expertise to determine if horticulture therapy would be an effective medium of treatment for individual clients. The therapist must also assess the appropriateness of specific activities given the client's needs and abilities.

This book is not a comprehensive horticultural guide. You will need to seek out additional information from the many excellent horticultural books and magazines found in libraries and stores, and to ask local gardeners for advice. The Resources chapter of this book is a good place to start.

You do not need to be an expert gardener to use horticulture therapy. Experiment with the ideas suggested here and adapt them to fit the needs of your clients and the resources available.

Remember to refer to the glossary if you come across unfamiliar words or expressions. You may also find other horticultural and medical dictionaries useful.

Chapter 1

>─┤◆┝─○─┤◆┝─◁

"Life Began in a Garden"

– inscription from a sun dial

Our environment affects our self-image, our motivation, the quality of our work, and our general health. Pleasant surroundings, indoors and out, can create a calm and happy atmosphere, and can help improve morale for your clients, for yourself, and for others working in your environment.

Plants and gardens help create pleasant surroundings in both obvious and subtle ways. The shade from a large tree gives welcome relief on a hot day. The cool green of a well-kept lawn soothes and relaxes us. Attractive vines subdue harsh concrete barriers. In the evening, the smell of a garden plant such as flowering nicotine is exhilarating. Sweet basil, with its delightful aroma, can help alleviate depression. These are only a few of the endless ways plants improve our environment.

The pleasant environment created by plants can induce a positive therapeutic response. In addition, horticultural activities offer your clients a chance to better understand the environment and themselves, to express their creativity and cultural heritage, and to develop and express caring, responsibility, and pride in a job well done.

The type of activities you use in your horticulture therapy program will depend on whether or not your clients are actively involved in gardening. This chapter defines active and passive horticultural activities and describes some of the personal and social benefits of gardening. It also outlines ways to use the indoor and outdoor areas of your institution as well as nearby public areas in your program.

1

Active Use of Gardens

"Active use" of a garden by your clients means that they are actively involved in establishing and maintaining plants. They may tend plants indoors in an atrium, in a greenhouse, or in some other area set aside for gardening activities. They may work outdoors on the property of the health care institution, in local parks, or in community gardens.

Active use of gardens gives your clients *physical* exercise and may be helpful in improving physical attributes such as hand-eye co-ordination, dexterity, and strength. Another important and often overlooked benefit is the positive feeling of tiredness derived from gardening. In many cases, people with disabilities have little opportunity to feel the natural, satisfying tiredness that comes from physical work. Many have to resort to tranquillizers and sleeping pills. Gardening allows your clients to get as much physical exercise as they need while doing an activity that is meaningful and rewarding.

Gardening can also improve your clients' *psychological* well-being. For many, these activities are something to look forward to, giving them a focus and feelings of success.

Finally, gardening can be *character-building*. It can help to give your clients a sense of responsibility and pride in their successes, and can teach them the value of patience and persistence.

Passive Use of Gardens

"Passive use" means that your clients are not directly involved in plant care. A palliative care unit is an example of a place where clients can experience gardens in this way. Indoors, passive use can range from appreciating a few plants in areas for reading and relaxing, to touching, smelling, and identifying the many plants in a large atrium (see Chapter 2 and Chapter 5 for additional ideas).

With outdoor gardens, ambulatory clients may go on walks, and clients unable to walk can be wheeled or assisted outside. Bedridden clients may be able to appreciate the outdoors through their windows.

> I haven't felt so worked out in years," smiles the willowy Twinka Thiebaud, a caterer in Los Angeles who abandoned her mountain bike and health club when she was told that gardening might work just as well. Unlike a jog or a sit-up, she found gardening is a purposeful exercise, a lung-cleaning, muscle-toughening activity that also decorates her house and stocks her pantry. "Every visit to the garden is the same," she says. "I'm just wiped out in a wonderful way."
>
> Time *magazine, 131, 25 (June 20, 1988)*

Outdoor areas can be inexpensively modified to increase visual stimulation. For example, bird feeders and bird baths will attract birds and animals and stimulate your clients' interest. (See Chapter 3 concerning wildlife or natural gardens and dream gardens.)

To make passive activities truly meaningful to your clients, you need to help them stretch their minds, to use their natural creativity and curiosity, and to learn new things. When you go on a walk or an outing, take a guide book along and identify plants, collect pine cones for Christmas craft projects, or take a group of children along with your group to add some extra energy to the experience (see Table 1).

Use of Public Spaces

You may be able to use municipal parks, natural areas, and other public spaces for your horticulture programs. Often these areas are accessible to the physically challenged, with such features as wide, gently sloping paths and washroom facilities for people in wheelchairs.

If you'd like your clients to garden in a park or other public area, talk to the manager of your municipal parks department. In many cities and towns, the parks department allows private citizens and groups to help create and maintain selected gardens.

When you meet with the manager, present a plan of how you and your group could contribute to the beautification of the park. Using such areas has valuable spin-offs such as increased social opportunities, a meaningful contribution to the community, increased environmental awareness, and the possibility of media attention for your program.

There are also passive uses of these areas. A walk in a park can be enhanced by collecting garbage for recycling, or by using your senses to appreciate plants: to feel rough bark, to listen to the wind in the trees, and to taste edible berries. Discuss possible activities with your clients. They may enjoy any number of things — berry picking, bird watching, plant identification, exploring a pond, photography, sketching, collecting material for crafts. Plan your outing to accommodate their interests. Also, do not restrict your activities in these areas to spring and summer: dress appropriately and enjoy the great outdoors throughout the seasons.

Social Benefits of Gardens

One of the best places to find people socializing is in a garden. It is easy to meet people in gardens, and gardening is an excellent topic to start off a conversation. The social aspect of gardening can be especially beneficial for people who are disabled because so often a

Table 1
Meaningful Walks

Where to Go	What to Look For	How to Use It
Institutional grounds	Landscape in winter. Red osier dogwood in dark shrub corners. Evergreens in planters form interesting shapes when covered with snow. Use of grey-green plants like sage to contrast against evergreens. Use of berry bushes and trees (e.g., vibernum, cranberry, and mountain ash). Bird feeders and seed-bearing trees.	Appreciate subtle colours; identify bird species; taste edible fruit.
Ditches, shrub borders, hedge-rows	Old jars, bottles, tins	Recycle to help maintain beauty of the grounds.
Just outside your window	Birds, insects, squirrels, trees	Look forward to changes in seasons.
Arbours, gardens, patios	Familiar and new plants	Identify common and scientific names using your horticultural resources.
Warm, sheltered spots	Plant growth in early spring	Many plants can be dug up, brought inside, and encouraged to grow.
Base of large trees, slopes	Cones, flowers, bark textures, squirrel caches	Experience coolness; experience power and strength of a tree.
Ponds, creeks, marshy areas	Insect, plant, and animal life	Bring back lots of samples and examine microscopic organisms in a lab.
Ravines	Old jars, dishes, kettles, and other odd and interesting items	Memory stimulation, treasures

disability causes isolation.

The flip side of this is the privacy a garden affords for institutionalized individuals who have few opportunities to be alone.

Gardening stimulates response, reaction, and involvement — all things that will, if encouraged and nurtured, eventually help to improve the health and well-being of people.

The following text examines three areas where horticulture can act as a catalyst to stimulate interest and involvement at every age: children's gardening programs, community gardens, and health care settings.

"Kinder-gardening"
Kindergarten is a German word that means "children's garden." For most children, kindergarten is the place where life in the real world begins. In the book *All I Really Need to Know I Learned in Kindergarten*, Robert Fulghum suggests that in this place we received the essential ingredients on how to live, what to do to make the world better, and how to cope if it is not going well.

Stimulation can be as simple as someone noticing a flower bud opening, a seed germinating, and roots developing. Children are very receptive to the changes that are an integral part of horticulture.

An example of "kinder-gardening" is the children's gardening program at the Teaching Garden at the Royal Botanical Gardens in Hamilton, Ontario (see pages 6–7). Beyond the excitement of starting plants from seeds and watching them grow, children make new friends and learn many lessons in co-operation, organization, and respect for the land and environment. The programs are fun for the children, and their parents enjoy helping.

Analogies, such as "plants are like kids," can be extremely useful in therapeutic activity with children. For example, the bird-of-paradise (*Strelitzia*) can take up to four years to flower, but when it blooms it is truly a sight to behold. This teaches children something about the bird-of-paradise, and also something about people — we mature at different rates. This is only one of several analogies that can be used when appropriate examples present themselves.

Gardening can teach children about the 4 P's: pride, patience, persistence, and practise.

Pride   Encourage them to take pride in the plants they are caring for, to see each plant as an individual with individual needs, and to feel responsible for the well-being of their plants.

> **B**e aware of wonder: Remember the little seed in the styrofoam cup: the roots go down and the plant goes up, and nobody really knows how or why, but we are all like that . . . "
>
> *from* All I Really Need to Know I Learned in Kindergarten *by Robert Fulghum (New York: Random House, 1988).*

CHILDREN'S GARDEN PROGRAM AT THE ROYAL BOTANICAL GARDENS

Each year brings a new crop of young gardeners to the Teaching Garden. Some 75 children participate in the program, which begins in April and ends in September. The only stipulation is that they be between 9 and 14 years of age and can attend regularly.

There are two levels of horticultural instruction. Children can attend for a maximum of three years — two seasons as junior gardeners, and one season as seniors, if their performance as junior gardeners merits advancement. The Teaching Garden Program is not connected with the curriculum of area schools, but the experience has proven beneficial in classroom studies.

In the junior program each member is assigned a garden plot of about 100 sq. ft. for which he is responsible during the season. The juniors are introduced to elementary botany associated with the growing of their vegetables and flowers. Instruction is of an interpretive nature. The subject is approached systematically in an attempt to foster a better understanding of the various aspects of gardening. Topics such as sowing of seeds, "pricking out" and transplanting of seedlings, cultivating, thinning, and harvesting of vegetables and annual flowers are covered thoroughly.

In many aspects the format of the senior program is similar to that of junior gardeners. Participants also study allied subjects such as plant diseases and insect identification, as well as the leadership qualities of senior gardeners.

Many of the vegetables, such as cabbage, broccoli, cauliflower, tomato, and pepper, are started indoors in an artificial-light garden. They are moved to the cold-frame area for a period to harden off before being transplanted to gardens. Students are taught to recognize named varieties of vegetables and flowers, and their individual qualities, merits, and characteristics. For example, it is important that they recognize that 'Explorer' is an early corn variety of good quality and appearance. Knowing these facts will assist them in planning their own gardens or those of their parents.

Each child is given a cropping plan that illustrates the size of the garden, planting depths, and distances between seeds and transplants, names of vegetables and flowers, and their position on the plan. Children are encouraged to follow the plan carefully, using it as a reference when planting their gardens.

From "Let's Get Growing" by Lynn Dennis, in The Gardens Bulletin 28, 1 *(March, 1974), a publication of the Royal Botanical Gardens in Hamilton, Ontario.*

Conservation is an important theme, and its importance is emphasized in such practices as crop rotation, succession cropping, and precision sowing of seed. The majority of plants are vegetables, with one row of annual flowers such as marigolds or zinnias for use in fresh flower arranging. Harvest is an exciting time, from the early spring radishes to tomatoes in late summer — taking home to the dinner table what one has grown on one's own.

Children are encouraged to utilize "waste products" such as beet tops either as food or compost. Composting is an important part of the season's activities; everyone contributes to a compost pile that will be used to enrich gardens of the future.

Children are taught the safe use of organic insecticides, and study life cycles of insects harmful to their gardens.

Wild flower and Native Tree Identification

Supplementing organized horticultural activities are nature-study programs. The children enjoy field trips where native wild flowers, trees, and shrubs are identified and studied in relation to their environment. For example, skunk cabbage (*Symplocarpus foetidus*), is found in swamp areas and flowers very early in the spring. The children are intrigued by its pungent odour and exotic flower. The finger-shaped leaves of sassafras (*Sassafras albidum*), together with the delightful odour and flavour of the bark and twigs, prove an interesting discovery on field trips.

Crafts and Culinary Arts

Through creative art, the children are encouraged to develop their imaginations in creating such projects as mobile sculptures made from odd pieces of driftwood, cones, and seed pods; floral designs of pressed dried flowers; and corn-husk dolls. Materials for art projects are, for the most part, collected from the wild. A session on dyeing, using natural dyes extracted from wild flowers and weeds, is a popular activity with the senior class.

The seniors are also given instruction in the culinary art of making jams and jellies. Cultivars such as black currant 'Magnus,' red currant 'Red Lake,' and gooseberry 'Captivator,' growing in the small fruit orchard, are picked, cleaned, and processed by the class. Everyone receives a sample jar for his efforts. The recently established demonstration orchard and vineyard will, in years to come, serve as an area where both children and adults can study the selection of standard and dwarf fruit trees. The area is used to illustrate proper orchard layout, and will serve to demonstrate the cultural operation and pruning of these trees. The vineyard, as well as the orchard, offers a selection of both newer and time-tested cultivars.

Patience   Growing a plant like the bird-of-paradise takes a lot of patience. For many children, even waiting the few days or weeks it takes for seeds to germinate will help them understand that some rewards take time.

Persistence   Any plant that survives neglect will show what can be done through persistence. The common dandelion is also an excellent example of persistence. It tries to grow almost anywhere and everywhere. In your lawn, it struggles after every mowing to produce new flowers and bear seeds; its leaves will even form a tight rosette and keep close to the ground to escape the mower's blade.

Practise   To be successful in gardening requires practise. Not everything can be done right away. Some projects take a bit of skill, but making the effort to learn to do new things and to do them properly has many rewards in the garden and in life.

The values of caring and responsibility can be reinforced again and again in gardening. Children can see how their plants thrive with proper care. You can help them to see how this applies to the way they treat themselves and others. Plants need someone to care for them — they need you! Being needed can be very important to children and adults who are lonely and depressed and receive little comfort from other people.

To thrive, plants need proper food, light, and soil. If plants are given too much or too little of these, they may weaken and die. But if care is taken to respond to their needs, they will flourish. This is a lesson that can be learned without the therapist, a lesson learned through the child's observations that could very well change the way he or she lives.

Community Gardens

Community gardens that are well organized and regularly supervised and maintained can be tremendously helpful in stimulating a sense of community in your clients. Community gardens are gardens where family, friends, or even members of various ethnic groups work together for common goals. The fruits of such labour may include socialization, lasting friendship, information exchange, and produce fresh from the garden. Gardens can also be built near sport fields, swings, slides, paths, and tennis courts to extend the social benefits to your clients.

Gardening not only allows your clients to express their creativity, it also allows them to express both their cultural traditions and their commonality with people of all cultures. Help your clients to integrate their individuality and their cultural traditions into their gardening activities. This will help increase their self-awareness and pride in their traditions. Interested clients may wish to design gardens based on their particular cultural heritage, to grow plants that are important in their culture, or to prepare ethnic dishes from their garden produce. For more information on community gardens, contact the National Capital Commission in Ottawa.

Horticulture in Health Care Settings

Making the exterior and interior of your institution more pleasant and friendly has been shown to be very valuable. D. R. Thoday and M. T. Sargent, in their book *Hospital Grounds Utilization,* investigated the social and medical contributions hospital grounds make to the hospital community. They found that well-designed grounds can directly serve patients, staff, and visitors.

Many people in institutions suffer from something that should not be a part of their treatment — boredom and a feeling of uselessness.

Our lives are made up of a series of small

A few years ago, in honour of the International Year of the Child, an ethnic garden was designed, planted, and maintained as part of the Royal Botanic Garden's Teaching Garden in Hamilton, Ontario. People from all over Hamilton were invited to participate that season. The Italians planted their broccoli, the French their garlic, the Chinese their cabbage, and so on. They tended their gardens in traditional ways, and they shared their expertise with the community of gardeners at the Teaching Garden. The ethnic garden was the scene of many social activities. Time and again, participants would arrive with family and friends and share garden news — "Our squash are in blossom," "Your tomatoes are nearly ripe. . . ."Nearly everyone who came left with something. Their trip to their garden was a meaningful one.

activities — achievements, really — repeated throughout the day, every day. If you take the routine away, life is full of uncertainty and success becomes more difficult. Horticulture has a very wide range of tasks that seem unrivalled for giving a feeling of satisfaction and achievement. For many clients, gardening can provide many small successes along the way.

For many entering the final stages of life, elemental things become very important. These elemental things might include interactions with plants, children, and music. Often, older people in the final stages of life have a sense of "presentness." In other words, they live each day to its fullest, knowing their time is limited. They have lived a long life and tend not to fear death. They are confused only by the death of people younger than themselves.

In nature, plants such as annual flowers and trees are often at their peak of beauty just before death. As with nature, there is often a peaceful beauty to the human spirit prior to death. This may be made even more precious and beautiful with plants.

Nature is generous in its efforts to preserve life. In spring, seedlings pop up everywhere, and in autumn there is a profusion of seeds. Plants can truly help us to see the realities of life, as well as death, and the continuity of succeeding generations, and the true meaning of heritage.

This chapter introduced you to the benefits of horticulture therapy, gave examples of some activities, and outlined the locations where horticulture therapy activities could take place. The following chapters expand on these concepts.

Chapter 2

❧ ⦿ ❧

Indoor and Greenhouse Gardens

Horticulture programs can take place indoors, outdoors, or in a greenhouse. Many programs use a combination of these three areas, but an indoor location is usually the most convenient and least expensive.

In order to begin, all you really need is a room with good light and some simple tools and materials. Indoor gardening is possible year-round. Winter days can become summer days with flourishing plants in a rainbow of colours, textures, and shapes growing in atriums, activity rooms, private residences, or anywhere stimulation and a change of season is needed.

Indoor gardening is often preferable for clients with limited mobility and is a good choice for clients with little experience in gardening. Some of your clients may never have had an outdoor garden, but nearly all will have had at least a few house plants at one time or another.

Depending on the needs of your clients and the resources available, indoor gardens can be quite simple, very elaborate, or something in between. This chapter looks at atriums, windowsill gardens, window greenhouses, artificial-light gardens, and traditional greenhouses. It suggests ways to increase the effectiveness of these gardens for horticulture therapy.

Remember that your clients are more likely to respond successfully to gardening if the plants flourish. This means that indoor gardens must have proper lighting, good plant selection, and regular maintenance. To ensure that these essential requirements are met, refer to the Resources chapter for books on indoor and greenhouse gardening.

Choosing Plants for Indoor Gardens

Plants should make the health care environment more pleasant, be easy to care for, and enhance the therapeutic experience. Plants can screen excessively bright sunlight, making an area more comfortable. They can soften harsh architectural lines, ugly barriers, and hallways, helping clients to forget that they are in an institution.

When selecting plants for horticulture therapy projects one should first consider the therapeutic value of the plants. This is discussed in greater detail in Chapter 5.

When selecting plants, remember that even greenhouses have limitations. The general-purpose greenhouse is expected to accommodate a wide range of plant material. Plants needing extreme conditions, such as high humidity, should be eliminated to avoid disappointment. Grow only plants that will tolerate conditions in your greenhouse.

For other indoor areas, select plants that are tough and can tolerate neglect yet still flourish. Many plants will grow well in extreme conditions (Table 2) and are good choices for problem areas in the indoor environment. Other plants will also tolerate the abuse and neglect prevalent in so many health care settings and still thrive and provide pleasure and enjoyment.

Plants that thrive on neglect can be useful in understanding life experiences. For example, one day my daughter brought home a sunflower seed in a container from school and placed it in our kitchen window. It struggled with varied temperatures, inadequate light, uneven watering, and the occasional spillage and replanting. She transplanted it outside. In the autumn, it produced a flower, and the ultimate goal was achieved. It had overcome adversity.

A plant like this can teach us much about our own lives. In fact, many plants can be used as analogies to help your clients, as well as having other therapeutic uses such as encouraging conservation and stimulating the competitive spirit.

Atriums

An atrium is an open area or courtyard within a building, usually under a skylight. Atrium gardens can range from a few plants grouped in a sunny corner to a large expanse with tropical trees near a babbling brook. Many institutions have an atrium that could be used as part of a horticulture therapy program.

An attractive, well-maintained atrium is not only an excellent place to care for plants but can also have important social benefits. Your clients and their visitors will feel relaxed and at ease. It is a comfortable place in which to visit. Hospital staff and others will often use it as a meeting point, making

Table 2. Indoor Plants that Thrive on Neglect

Name	Comments	Light	Water	Temperature	Humidity	Soil
Foliage House Plants						
Cast iron plant *Aspidistra eliator*	Virtually indestructible; regular fertilizing not necessary.	shade to half sun (east or southeast window)	keep evenly moist; let it dry out thoroughly between waterings in winter	13°–25°C (55°–77°F)	average	all purpose
Grape ivy *Cissus rhombifolia*	Hanging plant; pinch back periodically to keep it bushy; fertilize in spring and summer with fish emulsion or fertilizer such as 20–20–20.	shade to half sun (east or south-east window)	keep evenly moist	13°–20°C (55°–68°F)	average	$^2/_3$ tropical soil mix, $^1/_3$ sand
Mother-in-law's tongue *Sansevieria trifasciata*	Do not fertilize	shade to full sun (south or west window)	once a month; keep dry in winter	16°–25°C (61°–77°F)	average	all purpose
Flowering House Plants						
Kaffir lily *Clivia miniata*	Fertilize in spring to help it bloom.	partial shade	keep evenly moist; let it dry out in winter to encourage spring blooms	16°–21°C (61°–70°F)	average	loam-based
Lipstick vine *Aeschynanthus lobbianus*	Hanging plant; blooms throughout the year (at intervals); fertilize with fish emulsion or fertilizer such as 20–20–20 in the spring.	partial shade to half sun (east or southeast window)	keep evenly moist; let it dry out thoroughly between waterings in winter	16°–25°C (61°–77°F)	average	high organic matter (50% peat)
Peace lily, white sails *Spathiphyllum wallisii*	Blooms throughout the year; fertilize with fish emulsion or fertilizer such as 20–20–20 in the spring.	partial shade to half sun (east or southeast window)	keep evenly moist	18°–22°C (64°–72°F)	average to high	high organic matter (50% peat)

From "Grow Plants that Thrive on Neglect," *Canadian Living*, November, 1985.

the atrium a vital social area and giving clients many opportunities in which to interact with others.

Windowsill Gardens

A windowsill garden is easy and inexpensive to create. However, the temperature,

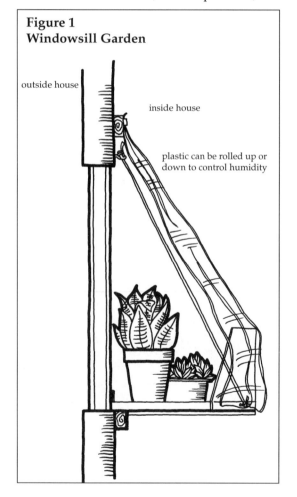

Figure 1
Windowsill Garden

outside house

inside house

plastic can be rolled up or down to control humidity

humidity, and ventilation will vary depending on the conditions in the home or institution. Some plants will not tolerate extreme variations.

Figure 1 shows a simple plan for constructing a windowsill garden. It can easily be made portable and can be adapted to most conventional-style windows. A wheelchair can fit under the shelf, allowing clients easy access to the plants.

The selection of plants for windowsill gardens and for window greenhouses should be based on the exposure or amount of available light (Table 2) as well as their therapeutic value (see Chapter 5).

Window Greenhouses

A window greenhouse is an extension of a window area (e.g., a bay window), usually with a southwest exposure (Figure 2). In a window greenhouse, garden maintenance is not overwhelming, and a great deal of variety is possible through imaginative selection of house plants, seed, and herbs. In fact, a window greenhouse is a great alternative when a full-sized greenhouse is not possible.

Although a window greenhouse costs more initially than a windowsill garden, it has several advantages over a windowsill garden.

- A window greenhouse has much

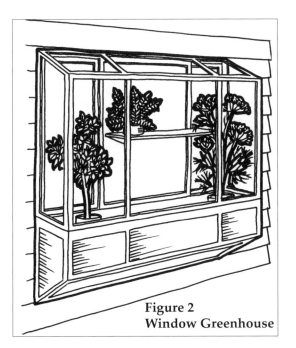

Figure 2
Window Greenhouse

greater flexibility in the types of plants that can be grown.

- You can create an environment similar to a terrarium in a window greenhouse. Because the climate is more consistent, seeds germinate faster and cuttings root faster.

- A window greenhouse can be constructed from floor level so that large interior plants, such as figs, palms, and bananas, can be grown.

A window greenhouse should be in a convenient location. In a home, this may be a frequently used area like the kitchen where a water source is available, but any southwest location is a good choice.

A window greenhouse is typically about 76 cm x 122 cm (2.5 ft x 4 ft) and will accommodate about 30 average-sized pots. It should be constructed so that it is easy for your clients to use. For example, clients in wheelchairs must be able to reach to the back of the shelves from a sitting position, so the shelf should not be deeper than arm's length, typically 75 to 100 cm (2.5–3 ft). Generally, a window greenhouse is attached outside a window facing southwest or southeast.

As in the case of windowsill gardens, plants should be selected based on light exposure and their therapeutic value, and should be given a quarter turn once a week.

Artificial-light Gardens

Plants can be grown successfully under artificial lights, and in certain situations, gardening under lights may be the best alternative. Using artificial light is much more convenient and less expensive than operating a conventional greenhouse. It is also a good choice for clients sensitive to natural sunlight. Because substance abusers and people on medication may become more aggressive under higher temperatures, gardening under lights is preferable to gardening in a greenhouse where temperatures can be relatively high.

The size, style, and cost of your artificial-light garden should reflect the needs and resources of your program. Figure 3 illustrates a homemade light garden with a metal frame, plywood shelves, and recycled 2.8 m (8 ft) fluorescent light fixtures mounted on adjustable chains and hooks. It was designed by the author to serve the needs of approximately 75 people. This particular design, with two or three tiers, 40-watt fluorescent lights, drainage pans, and an automatic timer, all set on casters, would cost approximately $300 CDN to construct.

Stands for artificial-light gardens can be built or purchased to suit your clients' needs for accessibility and convenience. For someone who is bedridden, a portable unit can be pushed up to the bedside or over the bed. If the client is ambulatory, the unit can be designed for convenient access from both sides.

There are some excellent commercially made stands, with specially designed units to fit over chairs and beds. Stands for artificial-light gardens can also be constructed for very little. In fact, they can be as simple as a shelf and a wooden frame with 1.3 to 2.6 m (4–8 ft) fluorescent fixtures on adjustable chains mounted on the benches. Information on types of lights, installation of lights, and plant selection, care, and propagation may be found in a number of good horticultural guides (see, for example, an entire chapter in the *University of Alberta's*

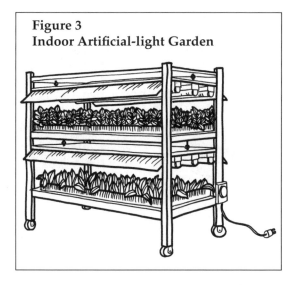

Figure 3
Indoor Artificial-light Garden

Home Gardening Course, which is listed in the Resources chapter).

Tips for Artificial-light Gardens in Health Care Settings

- Lights can be on a stand or in a permanent wall fixture.

- The artificial-light garden must have automatic timers installed to avoid having to rely on someone to turn them on manually. Day lengths can be predetermined using timers.

- Hospitals and nursing homes are often hot and dry, especially in winter. The artificial-light garden must have a method of retaining humidity, such as a clear plastic cover over the plants or a pan with pebbles and water.

- The installation of fans in the artificial-light garden can be beneficial and sometimes essential to maintain moderate temperatures around the plants.

Greenhouses

Greenhouse gardening also offers many advantages to your program. It stimulates your clients' senses with novel colours, textures, and smells, and it provides an attractive space where clients can focus exclusively on horticulture year-round. The relatively high humidity in the greenhouse may help clients with respiratory problems. On the negative side, high temperatures, noise from fans, vents, and misting systems, and other factors may make it a less than ideal work area. Greenhouses can also be relatively expensive to construct and maintain, and they usually require more knowledge to operate than simpler forms of indoor gardening.

There are many types of greenhouses: free standing, lean-to, cold frame, and the portable mini-greenhouse. Many excellent reference books, government publications, and manuals exist that can assist you in greenhouse design and gardening. The emphasis in this section is on modifications to accommodate people with special needs in a comfortable and productive way.

Greenhouse Modifications for the Physically Challenged

Figure 4 shows a greenhouse that has been modified to accommodate people with special needs.

Maximizing Comfort

A pleasant environment will achieve an optimum therapeutic response. Discuss the greenhouse experience with your clients to find out how it can be made more pleasant for them. For example, you may wish to turn off fans when your clients are working or visiting in the greenhouse to limit noise and confusion. If clients are in the greenhouse for extended periods, proper ventilation, shading, and temperature control are essential. If this is not possible, then a separate, comfortable work area near the greenhouse should be used.

Keeping Greenhouse Costs Down

Typically, we think of greenhouses as being made of metal and glass. Glass can be very expensive to install and repair when panes are broken. You may be able to obtain glass for a low price or for free if an old glass greenhouse is being torn down in your area. However, for horticulture therapy programs on tight budgets, wood frame and plastic construction is usually the best alternative.

To reduce heating costs, you may be able to supplement existing systems with solar devices such as barrels of water which heat

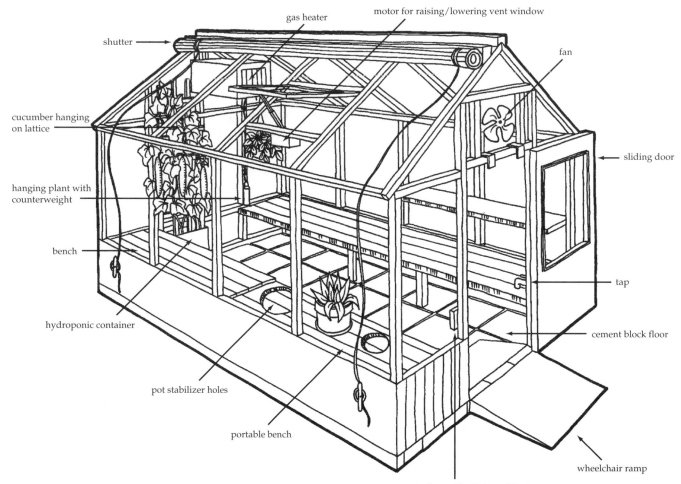

shutter

cucumber hanging
on lattice

hanging plant with
counterweight

bench

hydroponic container

pot stabilizer holes

portable bench

gas heater

motor for raising/lowering vent window

fan

sliding door

tap

cement block floor

wheelchair ramp

control panel for light and heat

Figure 4
Greenhouse

Table 3. A Checklist of Greenhouse Maintenance Activities

Activity	How Often	Suggested Therapeutic Objectives
Temperature Check Most greenhouses are thermostatically controlled. For the general purpose greenhouse, day temperature is usually 20°C (68°F), night temperature is 15°C (59°F)	Twice/day	Practise routine memory function. Environmental change from too warm to just right to cold makes patient aware of their comfort zone, as well as that of the plants.
Ventilation: manual vs. automatic.	Several times per day or as needed	Automatic ventilation is convenient, but must be monitored. Using manual ventilation encourages clients to inspect. Frequently, this helps develop a sense of responsibility.
Humidity Check Hosing down floors helps to maintain adequate humidity levels, helping to prevent plants from drying out.	Once/day in winter, twice during hot summer days	Increases strength to upper and lower extremities. Watering and using a hose improves balance and co-ordination for ambulatory patients. For the mentally handicapped, eye-hand co-ordination is encouraged. There is immediate gratification from the task. It is a fun activity!
Water Check Two areas: first, capillary action of propagation bench, and second, flats and pots of plants on benches.	Once or twice/day depending on crops, season, and number of plants	For mentally handicapped, repetition is pleasant and reassuring. Gratification derives from responsibility.
Trickle irrigation systems must also be inspected to see that all plants are being watered and fed.	Once/day	Fine motor co-ordination can be practised, having client insert "drip-feed" line to each potted plant.
Propagation Bench Check Automatically controlled heating cable should be checked for temperature set at 20°C (68°F).	Once/week	Young people who enjoy automation, timers, and adjusting dials, etc., could find a sense of responsibility in this job. It requires dexterity and practise.
Automatic mist system for rooting cuttings.	As required	A similar task, requiring a routine check while cuttings are rooting.
Fertilizing Check Mixture for automatic feed injector; manual feeding with water can. On-off switch on pump at water supply must be checked when feeding plants to see that fertilizer is actually being siphoned from reservoir.	Once/day, or depending on crop	Memory stimulation as recall; practise of fine motor skills, e.g., hand-finger movement.
Lighting/Shading Check Some greenhouses have supplementary fluorescent light. Lights should be turned off at night, especially if light-sensitive plants such as poinsettias are being grown.	Once/day	Automatic lighting improves sensory stimulation and perception, i.e., light = warmth; dark = cool. Useful in reality orientation. Controlling manual lighting aids in physical and mental dexterity, useful orientation for mentally frail and elderly.
Pest Control Check	Once/day or as necessary	Searching, finding, observing, and questioning skills are all practised. Hand lenses are essential.
Plant Maintenance Check Disbudding, pruning, deadheading, removal of dead leaves, washing foliage.	Once/day	Professional horticultural assistance may be needed in many of these procedures, but once mastered, clients will enjoy performing these activities. Fine and gross motor experience; also benefit to concentration; very relaxing.
Clean-up Check Washing pots to organizing storage shelves and stacking pots in order of size.	Once/week	Repetition of this work is very helpful for mentally challenged, promotes a sense of pride and responsibility in order and cleanliness.
Timing Device Check Very useful, especially in institutions. Activity is applicable to lighting, auto feed injector, and heating system.	Once in a while	For seniors who are experienced gardeners, this could be just the activity needed to develop self-esteem and responsibility. It demands a reliable person. With practise, reliability, memory, and concentration are developed.

up during the day and radiate the heat during the evening. Thermo blankets fitted inside the greenhouse which can be lowered inside the frame on cool days and overnight help retain heat. Another option is a passive solar greenhouse that uses water in large pails (about 20 litres, or 5 U.S. gallons) to store and slowly release heat.

Greenhouse Maintenance

It is preferable that the operation of the greenhouse be supervised by someone with a good knowledge of greenhouse management, maintenance, and cropping. Such a person would be familiar with such factors as ventilation, shading, watering, heating, and cleanliness that will ultimately determine the success of your program. Your clients can participate in various factors of greenhouse maintenance depending on their capabilities and needs. A checklist of greenhouse maintenance activities is shown in Table 3, along with their suggested therapeutic value.

This chapter described modifications to indoor and greenhouse gardens to make them more accessible and enjoyable for your clients. The next chapter outlines modifications for outdoor gardens.

Chapter 3

➤━◆➤━○━◀◆━◅

Outdoor Gardens

This chapter provides ideas for designing, modifying, and using outdoor gardens to make them more enjoyable for your clients, to stimulate their minds, and to encourage a response from them. Five types of outdoor gardens are highlighted: *production gardens, raised gardens* for the physically challenged, *gardens for the visually impaired, wildlife gardens,* and *dream gardens.* There are also ideas for growing plants in containers, often a good choice for the physically challenged gardener, and advice on accessories for outdoor gardens. Remember that modifications should be made a little at a time; gradual changes are less threatening and usually less expensive and less onerous.

As in the rest of this book, the focus here is on *adapting* gardens for horticulture therapy. For information on the principles,

plans and design, plants, and maintenance of outdoor gardens, see the Resource chapter. Many other books and magazines are available in your library or bookstore. Several books that specialize in garden design for the disabled are listed in the Resource chapter.

Basic Considerations for Outdoor Gardens

Outdoor gardens should serve the needs of your clients, challenging their abilities while limiting frustration. There are three major factors which need to be considered when designing or modifying outdoor gardens for horticulture therapy: accessibility, maintenance, and pleasure.

Accessibility   Accessibility will directly influence how and how often the garden is used. Your clients should be able to go to the garden often, preferably on their own. Once they are there, they should be able to become involved in some way, whether in gardening, exploring, or reflection.

The methods used to make the garden physically accessible will depend on your clients' capabilities. A person in a wheelchair may need ramped stairways, paved pathways, or water taps within reach. A blind person may need rails along pathways to serve as guides. Areas which are hazardous should be roped off. Talk to your clients about how to modify the garden to make it more accessible for them.

A garden must also be psychologically accessible. People who have never gardened or who have gardened only out of necessity may associate gardening with hard work, sweat, and tears. To make a garden accessible for them, it must also be nonthreatening. For example, if your clients find a large garden threatening, reduce the number and size of flower beds, or create small areas with shrub borders for privacy, giving the perception of greater security.

Maintenance   Regular maintenance is an important part of the gardening experience, and it is essential to make the garden an attractive and enjoyable place for your clients and others. If your clients are responsible for garden maintenance, the garden must be manageable for them in terms of its size and the degree of knowledge needed to maintain it. They must also be able to use the garden easily and on a regular basis.

Pleasure   A garden can provide your clients with the satisfaction of worthwhile physical labour. It can also be a place for valuable aesthetic and social experiences if it has an attractive design, stimulating plants, and amenities like benches for rest and reflection. As well, the garden should be as comfortable as possible for your clients. A warm southern exposure sheltered from the wind is an excellent site for early spring gardening activities. For those

> We all have an idea of a garden. It is the place where we wish we were, where we are at our best: generous, fertile, humble and at peace. For some the vision may be exquisitely formal, a garden of thought and geometry, traced with tulips and a perfectly taut hedge. For others it is wild and artless, with shaggy trees and hiding places and children splashing in clover. Even if we have never been there, we know what it looks like."
>
> *Nancy R. Gibbs, "Paradise Found: A Joyous Return to the Garden,"* Time *magazine, 131, 25 (June 20, 1988), 52.*

sensitive to direct sunlight, such as older people or clients on certain medications, the garden should include shade, with activities scheduled for the cooler times of day. Controlling insect pests may also be important to ensure that your clients enjoy their garden (see Chapter 7).

Paths in Outdoor Gardens

For some clients, the pathways in the garden will influence accessibility. Your client population and their degree of disability will help to determine whether paths are warranted. If paths are needed, they should be a minimum of 1.5 m (5 ft) wide and no steeper than a 6 percent grade. Steep paths can tire out clients and lead to accidents. (See Chapter 7 for more information on improving path safety.)

Variety in path surfaces, direction, and widths (provided the path does not become too narrow) can add

greatly to the interest, appearance, and versatility of the garden. Table 4 lists a range of possible hard surface materials and their advantages and disadvantages.

Production Gardens

A production garden is basically a garden, or garden crop, grown or used primarily for commercial sale. Many people, groups, and institutions are using horticultural crops not only for therapeutic benefit, but also as a revenue source. Greenhouse crops, field and forest production, and mushrooms are just a few examples of crops that can be grown for profit, providing vocational opportunities for special needs groups. Many excellent programs already exist, including: L'Arche Industries in Edmonton, Alberta; Twin Firs Greenhouse program in Clearbrook, B.C.; and the Melwood Horticultural Training Center in Maryland, U.S.A. These programs are usually very cooperative in sharing

Gardening has long been a popular activity and in many cases a profitable vocation for the mentally handicapped. A number of successful projects bear mentioning. One such program is the Twin Firs Greenhouse Project in Clearbrook, B.C. Over two acres of land are utilized as a production garden.

The products grown by the residents are sold locally. The 6,225 square metre (67,000 square foot) greenhouse produces annual bedding plants as well as a variety of house plants which are sold locally. Employment, self-motivation, a sense of accomplishment, and many more benefits are being realized through the success of this program.

Other programs in Canada include The Plum Coulee Project in southern Manitoba and L'Arche Greenhouses in Edmonton, Alberta.

Table 4
Hard Surfacing: A Summary

	Suitability for wheelchairs	Suitability semi-ambulant (canes, crutches, walkers)	Use on ramps	Availability	Ease of installation	Aesthetic appearance	Cost range	Regular mainte-nance requirements
In-situ concrete	good	good	yes	easy	easy/ do-it-yourself	poor; better with surface treatment	cheap to medium	not normally
Tarmac (asphalt)	good	good	yes	easy	fair/specialist	poor	cheap to medium	yes
Precast concrete slabs	good	varies	yes	easy	fair/specialist	poor	cheap to medium	prone to cracking and replacement
Reconstituted stone slabs	fair/ good	varies	yes	fair	fair/ do-it-yourself	varies with make	medium to expensive	none
Pattern pave	fair	poor	yes	fair	specialist	fair	medium to expensive	none
Interlocking concrete or clay blocks	good	good	yes	fair/ easy	fair/specialist	fair/good	medium	none
Natural stone slabs (york, portland, pennant, slate, granite)	good	varies	yes	diffi-cult	specialist	good	medium to expensive	none
Brick	good	varies	yes	easy	fair/ do-it-yourself	good	medium to expensive	none
Gravel	poor	poor/ good*	no	easy	easy/ do-it-yourself	good	cheap	yes
Wood: sleepers or decking and sawn log sections	poor	poor	yes	fair	easy/ do-it-yourself	good	medium	yes
Cobbles set in concrete	poor	poor	no	fair	fair/ do-it-yourself specialist	good	cheap to expensive	none
Bark	poor	poor	no	easy	easy	good	cheap	yes
Epoxy bonded resin/ aggregate	poor	good	yes	fair	fair/specialist	good	medium to expensive	not normally

* Results depend upon standard of laying and material specifications.
From Growth Point, *HT No. 125.*

information and helpful advice on how to start a production garden program, the tax benefits, and costs. Many local and provincial government agencies have complete listings on projects that exist in their area, and there are many opportunities for grants to help you get started.

Raised Gardens for the Physically Challenged

A raised garden is any garden that is at a convenient height for easier maintenance (Figure 5). Since working at ground level is difficult for many physically disabled people, raised beds are a good option. Raised beds are a form of container gardening (for more on container gardening, see page 30).

Raised beds have many other advantages.

- If the soil in the garden is poor, then thoroughly incorporating rich topsoil, compost, or manure to raise the garden will promote better plant growth.

- Raised beds can be used to divide up large gardens and create areas that feel more secure and intimate.

- Attractive raised beds can provide an interesting focal point in the garden.

- Raised beds are ideal for trailing plants like ivy, melons, and a host of others.

- They can be stationary, portable, or permanent (Figure 6), depending on your clients' needs.

- Raised beds can provide additional

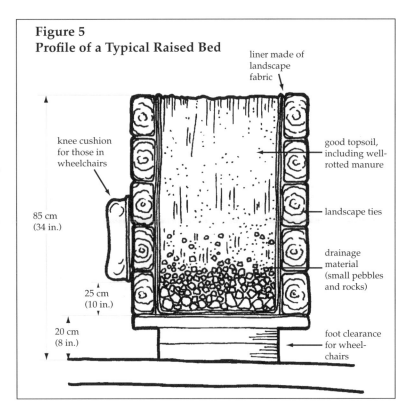

Figure 5
Profile of a Typical Raised Bed

liner made of landscape fabric

knee cushion for those in wheelchairs

good topsoil, including well-rotted manure

landscape ties

drainage material (small pebbles and rocks)

foot clearance for wheelchairs

85 cm (34 in.)

25 cm (10 in.)

20 cm (8 in.)

Figure 6
More-permanent Raised Beds

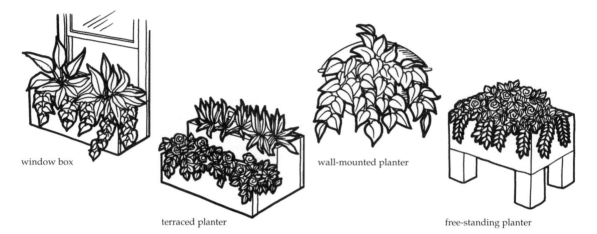

window box

terraced planter

wall-mounted planter

free-standing planter

Figure 7
Portable Raised Beds

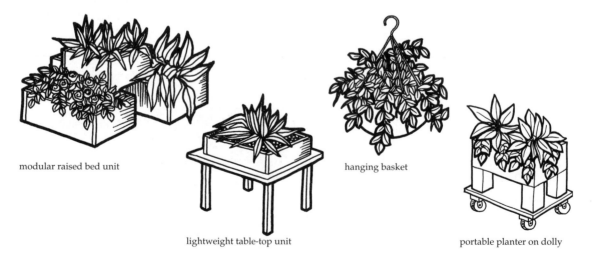

modular raised bed unit

lightweight table-top unit

hanging basket

portable planter on dolly

seating areas for both gardeners and visitors.

- Portable raised beds, mounted on casters (Figure 7) or set on a trolley, can be clustered for effect, brought inside if the weather threatens, moved if space is needed for other functions, or brought to a client confined to bed.

Design Considerations for Raised Beds
Assess your clients' capabilities and your resources, and work with your clients, their relatives, hospital staff, and volunteers to develop an effective, user-friendly raised garden area. It is a good idea to design a few prototypes and see which works best for your situation.

There are some basic factors to consider when designing raised beds for a horticulture therapy program.

Location   Your clients should be able to get to the raised beds easily. If possible, the beds should be accessible from more than one side.

The raised beds should be in a warm, sheltered spot with a south or west exposure, with adequate sunlight for healthy plant growth and adequate protection from wind for both the plants and the people maintaining them. The soil warms up faster and stays warmer longer in such areas, so use can be made of the garden from early spring to late fall.

You may also wish to put the beds in a quiet, relaxing area, but remember that an attractive raised garden should not be isolated or hidden. The garden's location should encourage its use, as well as create interest and stimulation.

Size   A small, well-planned, and well-maintained raised bed can be just as useful and effective as a larger bed. Choose a size that suits the space available, your resources, and your clients' needs. The reach across a raised bed should be no greater than 0.6 m (2 ft). For gardening from both sides, the ideal width of the bed is 1.2 m (4 ft).

Height   The height of a raised bed will depend on your clients' capabilities and whether they prefer to work while standing, sitting, or kneeling. A person in a walker may need a higher working level, while a small child may enjoy working closer to the ground. The beds should not be higher than 1.2 m (4 ft). If you have a number of heights for your raised beds, your clients can select whatever level is most comfortable for them at the time.

Water supply   Regular watering is essential since raised beds tend to dry out faster than ordinary gardens. The beds should be built near a water source. If possible, taps should be about 1 m (3 ft) above ground for people in wheelchairs. If hoses are required, a reel-type hanger is easiest to handle. In certain situations you may want to use trickle irrigation, but maximizing the automation may minimize client participation in this valuable activity.

Plants   Choose plants suitable to the particular exposure, soil type, and drainage. Also consider the therapeutic value of the plants. (See Chapter 5 for ideas.)

Seating   Benches built into or near the raised beds will provide a place for your clients to rest, socialize, and enjoy the garden.

Aesthetic appeal   Varying the heights of the raised beds can increase the attractiveness of the garden. You can soften the edges of raised beds by planting trailing plants like perennial alyssum, arabis, or ivy (avoid juniper as it is quite abrasive and may cause skin irritation). Raised beds will also look more appealing if they blend in with the landscape. For example, if wood framing has been used in the hard landscaping, retaining walls, and fences, then choose wooden ties

Table 5
Materials to Consider for Raised Beds

Material	Advantage	Disadvantage	Source
Metal frame	Durable, stable, portable	Harsh, care must be taken to make aesthetically pleasing	Metal shops, discarded pipe, scrap yards
Wood frame	Lightweight, economical choice in finishing	Must be treated	Recycled lumber
Peat bale	Useful to give temporary height to raised beds	May become saturated with water	Garden supplier
Brick, concrete block	Durable, easy to build; available at most construction outlets	Permanent, heavy, and hard to move; may not stand up to frost conditions	Old brick, construction sites, landfill areas
Plastic	Easily cleaned, portable, variety of shapes, commercially built	May crack or become brittle under extreme weather conditions	Hardware stores, garden centres
Railroad ties	Durable, usually inexpensive	Usually treated with creosote which can be toxic to plants; use old ties preferably	Railroad yards, garden centres
Natural earth	Using existing natural slope or bank of land; inexpensive	Hard to maintain; may not be available in your location	Institutional grounds, landscape contractor
Straw bale	Cheap, good for greenhouse cucumbers and tomato crops; useful for cold frames	May dry out quickly	Farmers, wildlife parks
Used items, e.g., bathtubs, sinks, tires, etc.	Creative ideas, cheap, easy to move, durable	If not well designed with appropriate plant material, may not be visually appealing; may need drainage	Garage sales, landfills

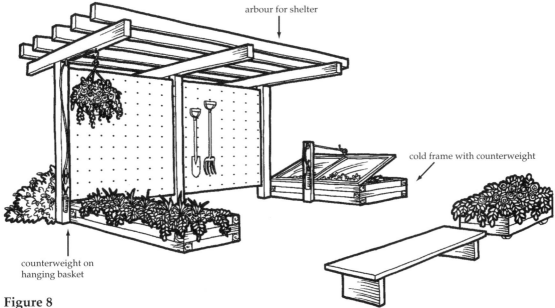

arbour for shelter

cold frame with counterweight

counterweight on
hanging basket

Figure 8
Example of a Modified Garden

or treated lumber as the construction material for the beds.

Wheelchair access   Modify the design of the raised bed so that clients in wheelchairs do not have to work sideways. The wheelchair foot rest should fit under the raised bed (Figure 5) and a cushion should be placed at knee-level on the raised bed to protect clients' knees.

Construction materials   Stability, strength, durability, weight, visual appeal, and cost are the key considerations in choosing appropriate construction materials for raised-bed frames. You may also need to

check building code regulations before making your selection.

Be certain that the materials are durable. In cooler climates, consider the effects of frost. In dry, hot places or moist and humid areas, rot may be a major concern, especially if you are using wood. Treating the wood with a preservative will extend the life of the bed, but ensure that the product used to treat the wood will not be toxic to plants. Also, remember to use extra care when choosing materials for large beds because the larger the bed, the more soil, and the more soil, the more pressure exerted on the sides of the beds. As noted above, the colour, texture,

GROWING IN CONTAINERS

Why Grow Plants in Containers?

- Containers can be arranged in groups and at different heights to make the most of any space or to create a working height that suits the individual client.

- They are small and relatively easy to maintain, although they do require more watering and feeding than ground-level garden plots.

- They are movable. Some can be mounted on trolleys or castors for easier moving. You can arrange them in different groups and take delicate plants indoors for protection.

- You can put them anywhere — on the windowsill, by the back door, on the balcony or patio, in waiting rooms, outside patients' windows, near garden benches and rest areas, as well as around the garden.

- Containers are very adaptable. You can create any soil condition, from marsh to alpine, and position them in sun or shade.

- They are versatile. You can change the plants throughout the year for maximum interest in every season. You can also use them for growing vegetables.

- They come in many shapes, sizes, and colours.

However...

- Watering is important. Clay containers dry out more quickly than those made of other materials. A gel is available which can be mixed with growing mediums to improve moisture-retaining qualities.

- Do not overwater. This is just as, or possibly more, harmful to your plants than underwatering.

- Plants in containers use fertilizer quickly, so they need regular feeding, preferably on a little-and-often basis, with a balanced soluble fertilizer with micronutrients.

- Weather conditions can be a problem. For example, hard frosts may crack containers and damage the roots of plants, especially those in clay and plastic containers.

Homemade Containers

Old oil drums, paint tins, boots, cisterns, stacks of tires, tea chests —anything that will hold soil and plants can be used as an interesting and unusual container. Old sinks provide particularly good containers for growing alpines.

Planting in Containers

Both used and new containers should be clean. Wash out any chemical or paint residues and old soil. Try painting used containers to disguise their original use. If needed, treat wood containers with a preservative and/or line them with landscape fabric to prevent soil from washing out their sides. When using paint or a preservative, check the manufacturer's instructions to make sure it will not damage plants.

The type of plants you wish to grow will determine the growing conditions you need to create within the container. Unless you want a bog garden, the container must have drainage holes. Without drainage holes, the soil will become saturated with water, and lack of oxygen will eventually stunt or kill the plants.

Having created drainage holes, you must stop the soil from washing out of them! Place a layer of stones or crockery (pieces of broken clay pots) in the base of the container. Over this rough drainage material, place a layer of finer stones. The depth of drainage material will depend on the depth of the container; generally, it should be about one-sixth of the total depth.

Modifications to a Typical Raised Garden Area (see Figure 8)

- Raised garden areas [approximately 0.75 m (2.5 ft) high] reduce excessive bending, allowing for ease in planting, cultivating, and harvesting.

- Hanging baskets placed at a 1 m to 1.5 m (4–5 ft) level are easier to water and fertilize.

- Lightweight plastic pots and watering cans are durable and easily cleaned and handled. Plastic detergent bottles control the amount of water applied to plants and are lightweight and easy to handle.

- Note that the potting bench, raised beds, and herb gardens are accessible from both sides, avoiding excessive reaching and lifting.

- Pulleys on cold-frame sashes make use of gravity in raising and lowering the sash for venting, watering, etc.

- Tools on the peg board are at arm's reach and stand neatly out of the way, but are easy to see.

- Note that the garden area is generally flat for ease in transporting materials and moving from one area to another.

- Bird feeders attract song birds to the garden area in winter.

- Plants growing on trellis structures are easier to reach and maintain. Examples of such plants would include roses, small fruits, flowering vines, and espaliered plants.

and style of the beds should be in harmony with the surroundings. Generally, the outside surface of the raised bed should be finished with a smooth, non-abrasive material. (Some ideas for designs are shown in Figures 6 and 7, and materials are listed in Table 5.)

Gardens for the Visually Impaired

With careful planning, you can create a barrier-free garden for the visually impaired. It is best to make changes a little at a time to avoid confusion and disorientation. It is also advisable to have your clients work in relatively small gardens so they can easily find their way around. Generally, three factors need to be considered when developing a garden for the visually impaired: guidance, surfaces, and interpretation and signage.

Guidance

Visually impaired gardeners need a guidance system to help them to find their way around the garden. The system should indicate points of interest like rest areas or fountains, alert the person to possible hazards, and mark locations of things like water taps and power sources. A combination of pathways, edging material and handrails, and other features that appeal to senses other than sight can work together to direct and protect visually impaired clients.

Rope is an easy and economical way to mark paths. Place yellow nylon rope (yellow is more easily seen by people with reduced vision) at about 1 m (3 ft) above ground, and knot it at important points (see Chapter 4, Table 6).

Edging the pathway with materials such as brick, boards no higher than 16 cm (6 in.), or strips of commercial plastic will help prevent the visually impaired from straying off the path, as well as acting as a sound guidance system when tapped by a cane or foot. An abrupt change in the texture of the walking surface can also be used to indicate special features.

Plants with unusual bark textures, fragrances, tastes, or shapes can be placed at important points along the path to orient the client. For example, fragrant herbs can be planted in beds exposed to the prevailing winds, or an aspen, with its rustling leaves, can be strategically placed by a bench. Other things that make sounds, like wind chimes or small streams, can also be used to mark features in the garden.

Surfaces

Surfaces for garden paths have been described in Table 4. Information on improving path safety is found in Chapter 7.

Interpretation and Signage

Interpretation is an educational activity which explains meanings and relationships through first-hand experience (see Figure 9). If you think in terms of interpreting a garden rather than just admiring it, a wealth of possibilities will open up for greater enjoyment of the garden. Here are some ideas for interpretation and signage for visually impaired clients.

Use of pictures   Laminated pictures can greatly improve the visual appeal of sign posts while communicating specific features and information to those clients who have some vision (see Figure 10). Unfortunately laminated pictures will fade more easily than other methods of illustrated signage such as painting.

Routed wooden signs   Wooden signs with large letters routed into the wood and painted in yellow can be very helpful. The signs can be read by tracing the letters with a finger. Yellow is easier to read for those with reduced vision. Paint is usually more durable than laminated pictures but painted signs are limited to short descriptions. The initial cost of routed wooden signs is high unless you have access to a carpentry shop that can make them inexpensively.

Brochures   Both Braille and Roman lettering should be used in brochures. Many people with reduced vision cannot read Braille but can read bold, large letters, 2 to 5 cm (1–3 in.) high.

Figure 10
Laminated Interpretive Signpost

Figure 9
Elements of Interpretation

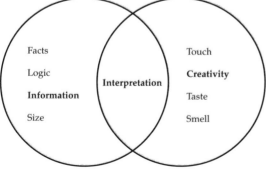

Facts

Logic

Information

Size

Interpretation

Touch

Creativity

Taste

Smell

Cassette tape and slide kits   These are usually very stimulating and visually impaired (as distinct from legally blind) individuals may find them useful. However, these kits are expensive to produce and maintain.

Interpretation includes both information on the subject to be interpreted as well as a creative method or approach in dealing with this information. For example, in interpreting the herb basil, we use both the facts that it is an annual and has aromatic and culinary value, and as well our creative abilities and senses in order to enjoy it.

Wildlife Gardens

Wildlife gardens are natural and unstructured areas. Flowers bloom at will, leaves fall and slowly decompose, birds and insects come and go — the whole garden flows with the seasons with little interference from humans. These

gardens can be especially satisfying for clients who spend much of their time in institutions.

For clients confined to beds or too frail to venture outdoors, viewing a wildlife garden can provide an invigorating change from a sterile, regimented indoor routine. For ambulatory clients, wildlife gardens are excellent places for meaningful walks (see Chapter 5). Clients can also do some garden maintenance, although this should be kept to a minimum to retain the garden's natural look.

Start your wildlife garden in a modest way with small changes to an existing area. Add a woodpile to encourage the growth of fungi and mosses or to attract blue jays, chipmunks, or squirrels looking to store seeds. Bird feeders, possibly made by your clients, can be set at a convenient height for maintenance, bird

Night-feeding deer, as some West Coast island and Prairie gardeners will appreciate, were a vexation to Japanese gardeners of old. It would not do to have a black pine, coddled and pruned to re-create the gnarled look of its wild counterpart, nibbled bare!

So the Japanese gardener crafted a clever device called a *shishi-odoshi*, or deer scarer (see Figure 11). A stout piece of bamboo about 1 inch (2.5 cm) wide and 25 nodes long was selected. One of the nodes near the center of the pole was pierced by a rod, which was mounted on another bamboo pole so that the shishi-odoshi would pivot. The long end rested on a stone; the short end had an open cup and stuck into the air.

Before leaving the garden, the gardener directed a trickle of water into the open end, which dropped when filled with water. When the water spilled out, the long end was once again heaviest. It then fell, striking a rock and resonating loudly enough to frighten away the deer. The cycle continues.

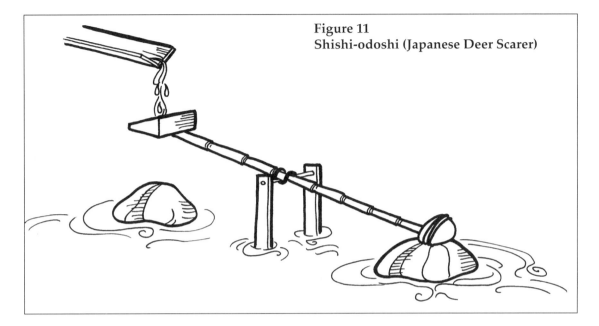

Figure 11
Shishi-odoshi (Japanese Deer Scarer)

watching, and safety from cats. A small pond or water fixture will attract birds and aquatic insects and increase the diversity of plant life. Incorporate seasonal interest into the garden by choosing plants that flower at different times of the year or are visually interesting all year long in terms of their winter bark or stem colour, fall leaves, or retained fruit. If possible, disguise or subdue the visual impact of artificial features, such as fences and retaining walls, by careful placement of plants.

Encourage input from your clients when creating and developing a wildlife garden. They may enjoy using the many nature books available to identify wildlife in the garden and to find new ways to encourage wildlife use of the garden.

Be sure to make provisions for garden maintenance. Although it should be low maintenance, some work will be needed to keep plants and plant debris from getting out of hand.

Dream Gardens

One of the most unusual and interesting gardens is the award-winning Hope Arena Garden, designed for recovering victims of head traumas at Moody Foundations Outpatient Clinic in Galveston, Texas. Here patients touch water, plants, and rocks, see movement and colour, hear water's different

Figure 12
Sketch of a Dream Garden

sounds, and experience an overall sense of peace. Landscape architect Keiji Asakura designed this garden based on Japanese beliefs about life and afterlife. Water ties the garden together and leads the patient through the Japanese view of life. At the garden entrance, a huge granite rock carved into a basin represents the womb. Water enters the garden through the womb. The water, trickling over brightly coloured pebbles catching the sun's rays, moves through life stages symbolized by grids of Pennsylvania blue stone. The grids represent how humans contour their lives to nature. Boulders placed in the stream represent life's difficulties. Just as the water swirls around the stone, a person rolls with the flow of life. Once past all of life's stages, the water passes through a portal and enters an attractive pond. The portal divides life and the after-

life. Fish in the pond represent new beginnings in the afterlife. The path should be designed so that the client returns to the starting point, perhaps in a figure-eight or oval design.

You can adapt the dream garden concept for your own uses (see Figure 12). For example, it can be a quiet, soothing area for confused, anxious, or mentally handicapped clients. Its features can be used as analogies in therapeutic discussions. Assistance from landscape designers can help you make the dream garden a reality.

Garden Accessories

A wide range of garden accessories, including fountains, arbours, bird baths and feeders, and garden furniture, is available to decorate gardens. These accessories can add the final touch to a garden, creating interest, stimulating conversation, and increasing the use of the garden. Select garden accessories with care, considering how their design, operation, and location will affect your clients.

Garden furniture should be functional, attractive, and durable. It will encourage clients and their relatives and friends to use the garden rather than an impersonal waiting area, and the change of scene will help to stimulate response, interest, and conversation.

Trellises and arbours filter sunlight and reduce wind speeds, protecting both people and plants from excessive exposure. There is also the beauty of the play of light and shadow on the surface below.

Lights and lighting are important for safety in dark areas of outdoor gardens. As well, lighting extends the use of the garden for visiting and relaxing into the evening. With careful consideration to lighting, the night garden can be made into a memorable experience. The fascinating effect of shadows cast by lights, along with the sounds of the night and the rich evening scents of plants such as flowering nicotine and roses, may have a sedative effect on someone who finds sleep difficult. The lights themselves should be placed so that they are hidden by plants, rocks, or structures.

Fountains and faucets add wonderful sounds and visual effects, while providing a cool retreat on hot summer evenings.

Garden ornaments can be effective, but ornamentation can easily be tacky or over-done. One has to decide when tastefulness and usefulness give way to gaudiness and distraction. A case in point would be the pink flamingo rage. However, if response is gained — and no doubt it will be — from celebrating a birthday with a flock of plastic pink flamingos in the garden, then it has been worthwhile.

Bird houses, baths, and feeders are probably the most useful ornaments for creating response. Birds in the garden stimulate interest, curiosity, and conversation.

This chapter described the design and modification of outdoor gardens for people with special needs. The next chapter describes ways to create and adapt tools to suit the needs of your clients while staying within your budget.

Chapter 4

‐◄►‐○‐◄►‐

Transforming Tools

Gardening, like any other task, is easier with the proper tools. Using awkward, ineffective equipment soon turns gardening into drudgery, and drudgery is not good therapy. Most therapists have two major equipment-related concerns when starting their horticulture therapy programs: how to meet the special equipment needs of physically challenged clients, and how to keep equipment costs down. This chapter will help you obtain efficient tools at a reasonable cost.

The first part of this chapter shows how you can easily and inexpensively adapt tools for use by persons with reduced strength or co-ordination, or a client in a wheelchair or walker, to allow them greater enjoyment and independence in the garden. The second part of the chapter gives you some ideas on

keeping equipment costs to a minimum, and focuses on recycling to create gardening equipment. By converting old milk cartons, margarine containers, coat hangers, and other common items into useful gardening equipment, you keep your costs down — and help the environment!

The suggestions in this chapter are just a start. By talking with your clients, you may create other innovative ways to meet specific equipment needs.

While reading this chapter or when your clients are working with tools, keep in mind a few words of caution.

- Most tools function best when the blades are sharp. You will need to evaluate your clients' capabilities to decide if they should use sharp equipment (for more information on safety, refer to Chapter 7).

- Help your clients remember two basic points when using gardening equipment: 1) Do not overdo it in the garden. Physical exercise is good, but not to the point of strain or exhaustion. Strain or exhaustion may result in accidents when using gardening equipment; 2) Choose the correct tool for the task. It will do a better job and take less effort.

Tools for Physically Challenged Gardeners

Hand Tools

Physically challenged people can sometimes use standard garden equipment as is. More often, a simple modification, like adding an extension onto a tool's handle, will make all the difference in the world to the disabled gardener. And if a piece of equipment must be made by hand, this in itself might make an excellent carpentry or craft project.

Table 6 lists common hand tools for gardening, ways they can be modified or made, and some sources for products and materials. This list is by no means complete. Work with your clients to find additional creative solutions.

More Hints

- Watering is by far the most important task in plant care, but it can be a difficult chore for many physically challenged people. Put casters on watering cans to greatly reduce the work of lifting and moving water. Smaller cans are better balanced than larger ones and are easier for clients to handle.

- Tools should be stored carefully so they do not cause accidents when not in use and can be found easily when required.

- Store equipment where it is easily accessible to your clients, giving them the freedom to use it independently. Signs or labels on shelves, cupboards, and peg boards may be helpful.

- A wooden A-frame plant stand can be a very convenient item (see Figure 13). It is completely accessible from all sides and can hold up to 20 pots or be filled directly with soil and drainage material. It can also be designed to accommodate standard plastic window boxes and can be used outdoors in spring and summer.

- An adjustable wheelchair garden table can be used over a wheelchair or an armchair (see Figure 14). The curved front rests on the arms of the chair and gives firm support to the user's forearm. A dowelling edge and a backboard help to keep soil,

Figure 13
A-frame Plant Stand

Figure 14
Adjustable Wheelchair Garden Table

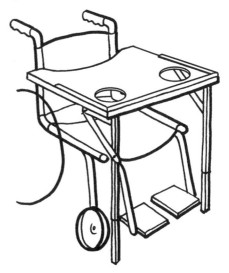

tools, and other items on the table. Holes of various sizes can be cut into the table top to hold pots while the client is potting seeds and cuttings.

- A walker fitted with a wire basket or a custom-built shelf between the handles can be very useful in transporting plants, tools, etc.

- People with good dexterity but not very much strength may enjoy a terrarium or windowsill garden using miniature tools. (See Chapter 2 for more information on windowsill gardens and other small garden areas.)

- If tools cannot be modified, your disabled clients may be able to work in pairs with one partner who is able to use the standard equipment. This can provide social benefits for your clients while giving their partners an opportunity to become acquainted with disabled individuals.

Remember, "If you think you can't do it, you're probably right."

Electric and Battery-operated Tools
A host of electric and battery-operated tools are available to the home gardener that may be helpful to physically challenged people. These tools are usually fairly lightweight and easy to service, maintain and store, and they do not require dangerous combustible

Table 6
Hand Tools and Adaptive Devices for Physically Challenged Gardeners

Tool	Commer-cial	Hand-made	Modifications and Characteristics	Advantages	Suggested Sources*
Homemade hand aerator	•	•	Handle at cane height, heavy metal base with tube. For extracting sod cores.	Doubles as a walking or support device while punching holes in the ground for aeration.	Mail order supplier
Pocket apron	•	•	Aprons with lots of pockets allow clients to carry an assortment of tools, materials, and supplies.	Easy access to tools, etc.; versatile; good craft project.	Department store, gift shop
Velcro® braces	•	•	Velcro® straps secure wrist and hand to garden fork. Leather cradle for arm with Fentex® straps and adjustable handle adapts to hoe, rake, etc. Hoe holder with wrist splint and Fentex® strap.	Useful if little strength in hands; encourages exercise in paralyzed arm of client in stroller; inexpensive.	Hospital's prosthesis department, medical supply company
Adjustable depth dibbler		•	Dowel of two different sizes: larger size to make shaft of dibbler; and smaller piece to insert at right angles to dibbler. Small holes can be graduated to varying depths so client can tell how deep to plant seeds and cuttings.	Inexpensive; useful for blind people or people with limited dexterity.	Dowel from lumber yard
Transport dolly	•	•	Can make or purchase dollies in various sizes. Use rectangular, square, or round 15 mm ($^1/_2$ in.) plywood for base. Commercial castors can be attached to dolly. Adjustable brackets will make dolly easier to manage.	Easier to move heavy items; avoids lifting and strain on back; good project for carpentry activity at nursing home.	Castors from hardware store
Garden fork	•	•	Standard garden fork with lightweight aluminum shaft and an added 'D' handle. Adjustable homemade 'D' grip is made from dowel and metal clamp.	Easier to use from seated position; leverage from seated position helps to counterbalance weight.	Garden fork from garden centre; dowel from lumber yard

* For a list of suggested suppliers, see the Resources chapter, or contact your University horticulture department, horticultural society, or a reputable horticultural supplier.

Tool	Commer-cial	Hand-made	Modifications and Characteristics	Advantages	Suggested Sources
Grabber	•		Approximately 1 m (3 ft) long.	Easier to retrieve flower stems and branches; especially useful for harvesting cane fruit, roses and other barbed plants.	Hardware store, novelty shop
Curved-neck hoe	•		Shaft is bent at base. Also elongated, with handle grip.	Allows hoeing and/or raking from upright position; prevents excessive bending and straining.	Mail order supplier
One-step hoe and tamper	•	•	C-shaped tamper welded onto back of hoe. Can be used to firm a transplant after hole has been dug, or to loosen roots of weeds.	Reduces need to bend and avoids strain on lower back.	Hoe from hardware store
Bulb planter	•		Metal cylinder is inserted down to desired depth, then pulled up. Soil core is then removed with metal insert.	Eliminates bending and stooping to plant bulbs.	Mail order supplier
PVC® tube planter	•	•	Ordinary 10 cm (4 in) PVC® tubing cut to approximately 1.3 m (4 ft) length. Can be used as a device to transplant seedlings or cuttings grown in peat pellets.	Inexpensive; easy to make.	Plumbing shop, hardware store
Cake dish propagator		•	Commercial cake or sandwich tray with attached handle can be used to start seeds and plants. Moisture and humidity are retained, while seedlings get ample light. A heating pad set on low provides bottom heat useful in seed gemination and root development. Use a hot iron to make holes in sides and top for air circulation.	Cheap; lightweight.	Catering service, bakery, department store

Tool	Commer-cial	Hand-made	Modifications and Characteristics	Advantages	Suggested Sources
Long-handled pruners		•	Convert garden secateurs to long-handled pruners by taping dowel to handles and inserting hand grips at operator's level.	Inexpensive; good for pruning at varying heights and in dense shrubbery.	Dowel from lumber yard
Pulley for raising and lowering plants		•	A simple pulley mounted to wall bracket, and a chain or rope attached to hanging plant on one end and knotted to the level desired. Makes watering of hanging plants very easy.	Avoids excessive reaching and lifting; fairly easy to assemble.	Hardware store
Scooper-rake		•	Two old bamboo cane rakes bolted together so they operate with scissor action.	Useful for gathering leaves and debris; lightweight; helps to reduce bending and strain; inexpensive.	Rakes from garage sale
Knotted rope		•	Use yellow plastic fibre rope and knot at intervals where you want a transplant to be planted or to designate where an object of interest is located.	For someone with limited vision, the knot indicates where plant is to be inserted into soil. The yellow colour is best seen by visually impaired people.	Hardware store
Ratchet cut secateurs	•		Pruning shears with ratchet.	Easy to grip; makes cutting through tough rose canes and tree branches easier; less strength needed in hand muscles.	Mail order supplier
Funnel tube seeder		•	Clear plastic tubing and a plastic funnel. Useful for planting larger garden seeds such as corn, peas, and beans from a standing position.	Eliminates bending; good for children and others who do not like to bend or touch soil initially.	

Tool	Commer-cial	Hand-made	Modifications and Characteristics	Advantages	Suggested Sources
Hand seeder with battery-operated vibrator	•	•	Tape hand seeder onto lightweight handle to enable client to reach across soil flat.	Inexpensive; allows for extended reach with ease. Seed tapes are also useful.	Mail order supplier
Rotary seeder	•		Approximately 1 m (3 ft) long.	Allows seeds to be distributed easily across flat; especially useful for sowing fine seeds; allows client to seed row from standing or seated position.	Mail order supplier
Long-handled loppers	•		Lightweight aluminum shaft with plastic grip handles.	Lightweight, durable pruning instrument.	Nursery or garden centre
Pot stabilizer		•	A handy tray with varying sizes of recesses allows client to pot seeds and cuttings from wheelchair position. Tray clamps onto arms of chair.	Stabilizes pots and takes weight of soil; convenient.	
Kneeling stool	•	•	Simply constructed from scrap wood. Helps client with reduced flexibility get down to plant level, and cushions knees and arms. Turned upside down, it can serve as resting stool.	Lightweight; inexpensive; stable.	
Lightweight terrarium tools	•	•	Miniature tools for bottle gardens are sometimes easier to use for clients with little strength. The handles are made of bamboo, with wire, sponge, and razor blade accessories.	Inexpensive; interesting to design and make; convenient for portable light gardens or windowsill gardens.	Garden centre, hobby shop

Tool	Commer-cial	Hand-made	Modifications and Characteristics	Advantages	Suggested Sources
Plastic tools	•		Child-sized tools made of plastic with wooden handles are very useful to clients with little strength in their forearms or who are confined to wheelchairs or beds.	Inexpensive; convenient size; lightweight; for indoor or outdoor gardening.	Department store
Trowel	•	•	Trowel with built-up handle made from pipe insulator is easier to grip and cushions tender hands. Trowels can be purchased commercially that are anatomically designed to fit the shape of the hand.	Inexpensive; easy to make.	Garden centre
Trowel with extended handle		•	Attach garden trowel to extended handle.	Depending on length of handle, tool can be operated from a standing or seated position; avoids excessive bending and kneeling.	Garden centre
Dish tray waterer	•	•	Place potted plants on dish drain with tea towel hanging into sink of water. Towel will keep moist and plants will not dry out. Useful as a plant caretaker.	Convenient when regular plant maintenance is difficult because of holidays and weekends; simple; inexpensive.	Department store
Lightweight wheelbarrow	•	•	Wheels counterbalanced for ease in lifting and moving.	Large wheelbase takes weight of load, counterbalances handle.	Mail order supplier
Cord wrap		•	Easily made out of scrap wood. Light-weight cord wrap allows both hands to assist in collecting cord and twine from the garden.	Does not require fine motor co-ordination; helpful for clients with good arm mobility but limited hand function; good carpentry project.	

Tool	Commer-cial	Hand-made	Modifications and Characteristics	Advantages	Suggested Sources
Rake on wheels 	•		Wheels aid in backward-forward motion used in raking.	Useful for people raking from wheelchair position	Commercial

fuels. Nursery and garden centres can give you information on the selection of electric and battery-operated equipment available in your area.

When considering electric and battery-operated tools, first evaluate your clients' needs and capabilities. For example, using a hand tool instead of an electric tool might give a client some much-needed physical exercise. As well, remember you can only reach so far with electrical equipment. Usually cords come in 15 to 30 m (50–100 ft) lengths. Safety precautions for using electric tools are discussed in Chapter 7.

Keeping Equipment Costs Down

New Equipment

Be sure to do lots of comparison shopping whenever you buy new gardening equipment. Remember that many retailers will give discount rates

and special service to nonprofit institutions. Also, some manufacturers might consider a donation to your institution as a way of advertising their products, especially if you are well prepared and enthusiastic when you talk to them about the value of your horticulture therapy program.

Garage sales are excellent sources of used tools and equipment.

Transforming Junk into
Gardening Treasures

"One person's junk is another's treasure" is a familiar adage, and it's true! Many "treasures" are thrown away every day. You can find them in an alley, at the dump, along the road — almost anywhere. Creative people look for the unusual. Sometimes creative people have to risk looking unusual to find the unusual, but the payoff can be tremendous. If we reuse other people's junk to serve a useful purpose, then we're setting a good example by helping to improve our environment and making effective use of our resources. Table 7 suggests ways to transform many inexpensive, easy-to-obtain items into treasures for your horticulture therapy program.

This chapter described many ways to adapt tools to suit the needs of your clients and provided ideas for creating tools from used items. The following chapter looks at activities and concepts you can use in your horticulture therapy program and gives examples of such programs.

Table 7
Creating Gardening Equipment from Junk

Item	Description	Suggestions for Use	Sources
Bread bags	Plastic, clear	Storing fresh cuttings; wrapping cuttings to be rooted.	Home
Floral baskets, wreaths, and arrangements	Wire frames, wreaths, wicker baskets, oasis and sphagnum peat that is usually discarded	Wire frame and sphagnum moss in wreath can be used again; ribbon and florist wire are reusable; baskets with "everlastings" can be bunched and used in new arrangements; in some cases, foliage like heather can be dried; oasis can be used to rearrange flowers; baskets might be useful as storage containers.	Garbage collection site, cemetery (with permission), landfill site, hospital
Margarine containers	Yellow, easily seen by those with partial sight	Good for storing small quantities of fertilizer. If used for rooting cuttings, drainage holes are needed; to aid clients with reduced vision, rectangular openings may be cut around outside circumference of lid as a guide for inserting cuttings.	Home
Egg cartons	Paper egg cartons	Cartons are quite absorbent; seedlings can be transplanted into carton and then each unit can be broken apart and transplanted into the garden as is.	Home, restaurant
Milk cartons	Waxed cardboard and plastic	Starting seedlings (remember to provide drainage holes!).	Home, institution
Oasis foam	A useful accessory when making fresh or dried floral arrangements because they are so very light. People with poor co-ordination may find them frustrating. If a small amount of sand is placed in a sandwich bag and laid in the base of the basket before inserting the florist foam, it is much more stable and less likely to tip.	Used oasis can be dried and moistened for at least one more flower arrangement; pieces can be broken and jammed into a jar for bouquets. Moist oasis can also be frozen and thawed out as needed.	Cemetery (with permission), dump site, home, garbage collection site, funeral homes, florist shop discards

Item	Description	Suggestions for Use	Sources
Rubber gloves	Commercially available; should fit snugly for better grip; yellow preferred for visually impaired	Handy for mixing soil by hand, for spraying in the garden, for washing pots, and for general clean-up in activity area.	Home, hospital
Coat hangers	Metal, cut and formed into stand for label	A straightened coat hanger serves as a sturdy stand for plant labels.	Home, office, dry cleaner
Plastic labels	Plastic labels received with gift plants, trays, and garden cell packs	Can be cleaned to remove original wording using fine steel wool, and then reused. Some garden centre labels have useful information printed on them; punch hole at tip and insert on wire stand.	Garden centre, garbage collection site
Peat moss	Peat moss used as packing material with bulbs, garden plants, etc.	Can be dried and reused to store crops such as carrots or tender bulbs for the winter.	Garden centre, commercial greenhouse
Translucent plastic pails, containers, bottles	Translucent materials are preferred so as not to burn tender transplants	Once cleaned, translucent vinegar jars and windshield washer containers make super hot caps for use in the garden in early spring because they allow sunlight to penetrate. Cut out the bottom and insert a bamboo rod through the top and into the earth to support jug.	Home
Pencils	Pencil stubs inserted in foam	Push stubs through lightweight plastic ball or sponge; for use by clients who have difficulty in grasping pencils.	Pencils from home, office; balls may be purchased

Item	Description	Suggestions for Use	Sources
Yellow plastic	Tags cut from yellow ice cream pails or other plastic containers	Yellow naturally attracts greenhouse pests, especially white fly, so yellow plastic strips make a good, environmentally safe pest control method. Cut plastic in strips. Punch a hole at top of each strip to suspend it. Paint strips with sticky substance like Vaseline or oil. Hang the strips in greenhouse area.	Recycled household items
Flower pots, flats, and trays	Plastic or clay pots, plastic flats	Pots can be washed and disinfected with household bleach, then stored for future use; plastic flats and pots are lightweight so are easier to use for people with little strength in their hands.	Garage sale, home, garden centres (look especially in late spring after bedding plants have been sold)
Nylon stockings, pantyhose	Onion bags, old nylon stockings; strong, yet allow air to circulate	Very useful for storing garden bulbs like gladioli and tulips to cure because they allow air to circulate; can also be filled with soil mix and used as planters.	Home
Juice tins	Large juice tin; solder copper tubing as handle and spout	Create a durable, lightweight watering can — and a real conversation piece — from a large juice tin and copper tubing.	Home, restaurant
Toothbrushes, tongue depressors, razor blades	Wooden tongue depressors, old tooth-brushes that have been sterilized, razor blades (ejector type)	Old toothbrushes are useful for removing scale from pots and insects from plants; tongue depressors can be used as plant labels; razor blades taped to bamboo stakes are good for pruning flowers and leaves from house plants. All of these items should be washed thoroughly and placed in boiling water for several minutes before using.	Home
Baking and cooking utensils	Metal pans, plastic trays, old mixing spoons	Old bread pans, bowls, etc., can be used as watering cans, storage containers, and for mixing soil; old cookie trays are useful to set plants on for watering; a meat baster is good for watering plants in pots and terrariums.	Home, restaurant, garage sale

Item	Description	Suggestions for Use	Sources
Yard and garden waste	Compost-type materials	Branches or twigs are useful to support vegetable crops, such as beans and peas; branches can be sprayed white and decorated for Christmas and other holidays; leaves and grass clippings are good mulches.	Home, yard

Chapter 5

><>◦<><

People, Plants, and Programs

Gardening is popular worldwide, and second to walking is the most popular pastime in North America. It is satisfying physical exercise, produces tasty vegetables and fruit and beautiful flowers, and creates a sense of community and personal well-being. Plants remind us of the cycles of life, from seed to harvest, and of renewal and regeneration. Gardening makes people more aware of the beauty of the physical world. They begin to touch, taste, see, and smell more acutely. An interest in gardening draws people together, initiating conversation and laughter. The garden is also a place to seek solitude in an institutional setting. For many people, the garden becomes a place to go when they need time for personal reflection. Most avid gardeners believe that their passion is profoundly good for them, and gardeners often live long, stay healthy, and generally keep happy.

The reasons for gardening's general popularity are also the reasons for its value as therapy. This chapter describes concepts useful in horticulture therapy, such as selecting appropriate plants, using plant analogies, and increasing the social benefits of gardening. It also gives examples of horticulture programs and activities.

To use horticulture therapy to its fullest potential, you have to sleep, eat, and drink horticulture! It is not just a case of memorizing a few facts and a few quotes. It requires research, thought, and remembering and using what you read, hear, and see in your program. Take the ideas in this chapter, do more research, and develop plans with your clients to create an effective program.

Your Clients

Limit the size of your horticulture therapy group to a manageable size. For most activities, there should be a 1:2 ratio of volunteers and staff to clients. If there are too many clients, individuals will not receive enough attention and the experience will become confusing and frustrating.

Discuss the program ahead of time with prospective participants to judge their level of interest and their view of horticulture. Although horticulture is a valuable therapy for most people, it is not for everyone. People who have never gardened or who gardened only out of necessity may associate gardening with hardship and hard work. You will have to use your judgement to decide on the degree of involvement of such clients.

If a client is or has been a keen gardener, encourage this person to participate. They will usually be a catalyst for others and can provide advice and assistance to less-experienced gardeners.

Some may only want to watch others or appreciate the activity from a distance. This should also be accepted as useful to that client, to others who participate more actively, and to the caregiver.

Soil

The importance of helping your clients respect and understand the value of soil cannot be overemphasized. Soil is a wonderful substance, a complex blend of organic and inorganic materials. It is filled with life, from tiny bacteria and fungi to earthworms. They break down plant residues and other organic materials, making nutrients available to plants and improving the soil's structure. Soil provides the growing medium for plants, the plants we depend on directly and indirectly every day of our lives. Encourage your clients to call it "soil" or "earth," *not* "DIRT." Dirt is found under the carpet. Soil is what plants grow in. Help them to appreciate the feel and smell of soil, and its true value.

Choosing Plants

Just as you need to get to know your clients, you must also get to know your plants. This will help you both understand what your clients are working with and develop and improve your program. Although cultural requirements are briefly outlined in the tables that follow, you will need to do further research, preferably of a "hands-on" nature, for complete information. You may find it helpful to keep a few good gardening books (see Resource chapter) on hand or a record of your plants' cultural requirements that you, your volunteers, and your clients can refer to when problems arise with particular plants. A recipe card box or a

TIPS ON HOW TO WORK MORE SUCCESSFULLY WITH YOUR CLIENTS

Use the 3 L's of friendship   Try to cultivate a friendly relationship with your clients. *Look* for similar likes and dislikes. *Listen* — just listening can mean so much to someone who is lonely. *Love* flows from concern.

Provide reassurance   Reassurance comes from the words spoken and the tone of voice, and from physical actions like a gentle squeeze of the hand, a hug, or a pat on the back.

Praise   Appropriate compliments and recognition help to retain interest and enthusiasm.

Encourage initiative   Be alert to any signs of initiative like spontaneous watering of plants, sweeping, or sorting. Then gently guide the activity to a productive outcome.

Speaking   Speak slowly and clearly with direct eye contact. Speak a little, then allow your clients to speak.

Be organized   Start small and work up. Have a plan and follow through. Do not rush.

Assess progress   Develop a method to measure progress. It need not be refined and clinical, but it will provide valuable documentation for enhancing or changing your program.

Physical activity in moderation   Physical exercise is important, but be sure your clients do not overdo it. Design activities to minimize bending, stretching, and lifting. Encourage clients with reduced strength to slide or push items rather than lifting and carrying.

Sensory stimulation   Plants, especially herbs and plant parts like bark, roots, seeds, leaves, beg to be touched, smelled, and tasted. Be aware of and use these natural stimulants in your activities.

Play on positives   If plants are neglected or diseased, discard or isolate them until they have regained health. Replace disappointment with hope.

Involve everyone   Watch for boredom and quickly change or refocus the activity. Allowing your clients to become involved in setting objectives and planning activities will minimize this problem.

Be alert to changes   Watch for forgetfulness, fatigue, restlessness, or drug effects that might affect the performance of individuals or the group as a whole. Activities punctuated with rest periods, refreshments, songs, and exercise will help to keep clients interested and aware.

Value every task   Consider each activity, no matter how insignificant, a means to an end. For example, mundane tasks like washing and stacking pots prevent the spread of disease and reinforce a sequence of events while encouraging order and stability.

Involve everyone in clean-up   Clean-up is just as important as the activity. It indicates the conclusion, defines the activity, and reinforces the accomplishment.

Have fun   The opportunity to have fun should never be overlooked. Every so often, stop and ask people if they are enjoying themselves. Laugh and encourage laughter — it is good therapy too.

3-ring binder may be useful for this.

Table 8 includes plants that are of particular value for horticulture therapy programs. Each of the plants has special characteristics that stimulate attention, initiate conversation, tease the senses, or create ongoing interest and enjoyment. With a little research, you can find other interesting characteristics of these plants, such as their historical background, folklore, or unusual uses. This list should not limit the plants you can use. Try using this same format to document additional plants so you have a record of their basic cultural requirements and the characteristics that initiated responses.

Level of Difficulty

For beginning gardeners, it is best to choose plants that are easy to grow. Once you and your clients have become more familiar with growing plants and need more of a challenge, then try some of the tougher ones. Where regular maintenance is a problem, choose plants that can withstand neglect (see Table 2).

Stimulation of the Senses

Plants with unusual smells, colours, leaf patterns and shapes, or unusual habits that stimulate clients are very useful in producing therapeutic responses (see Table 9). Table 10 lists some plants for atriums that are especially valuable for therapeutic purposes.

Hazard

Some plants are poisonous or hazardous in various ways. These plants *must* be handled with caution, especially when working with clients who like to handle and taste everything. When you start up your program, you may want to avoid these plants. Chapter 7 includes more information on hazardous plants.

Plants as Analogies

Using plants as analogies to human life can make the garden more meaningful by helping your clients to better understand themselves.

Consider the apple tree. The older it is, the more beautiful it becomes. With its twisted trunk, flattened top, and gnarled branches, it brings back memories and feelings of happiness. By its very presence, we remember its more productive years. Each branch is a living testimony to its years of productivity, just like your own family tree.

Using analogies also stimulates responses. For example, a simple way of achieving response with children is to pretend. Giving plants human characteristics (such as "strong" or "fragile"), or imagining plants responding to anger, or showing pleasure or regret, can help children come to terms with their own emotions, problems, frustrations,

Table 8
Plant Materials Valuable in Horticultural Therapy Projects*

Plant Material Scientific/Common name	Type (w = woody, b = bulb)			Use in Your Hort Therapy Program						Season for Use				Location		Ease of Growth (1 = most difficult)	Comments and Special Features
	Annual	Perennial	Biennial	Plant Propagation	Floral Art	Terrariums	Forcing	Garden Design Features	Craft Projects	Spring	Summer	Fall	Winter	Indoor Plants	Outdoor Plants		
Amaryllis *Hippeastrum* hybrids		b		•	•		•			•			•	•		2	A must for all horticulture therapy programs; blooms are spectacular, initiating competition for largest flower; wonderful as gift plants; clients are proud of these.
Begonia *Begonia rex* hybrids	•			•	•	•					•	•	•	•		2	Propagation is the main focus; roots will develop along veins by leaf lying on moist sandy surface; very tactile; hairy underside; pronounced veins.
European weeping birch *Betula pendula* 'Gracilis'		w			•		•	•	•	•	•				•	3	Analogy: "The Beauty in Weeping"; majestic; branches easily woven into wreath forms.
Bittersweet *Celastrus scandens*		w		•	•		•	•	•		•				•	3	Excellent as vine/groundcover; climber is not used as much as it should be; berries are the outstanding feature; vine can be woven into wreaths.
Chives *Allium schoenoprasum*		•		•	•							•	•	•	•	3	Garden herb; appealing to taste, sight, and smell; useful in cooking, salads, etc.; forced in winter.
Coleus hybrids *Coleus hybridus*	•			•	•	•			•	•	•	•	•	•	•	3	Easy rooting any time of year; seeds easy to germinate; wide range of spectacular colours coupled with a variety of leaf serrations.
Maidenhair fern *Adiantum tenerum*		•		•	•	•								•		2	Useful in terrariums; propagation by spores or root division, the latter involves an aggressive approach, tearing roots apart.

* Some of these plants may not be hardy in extreme climates but may be successfully grown in protected areas or indoors.

Plant Material Scientific/Common name	Type (w = woody, b = bulb)			Use in Your Hort Therapy Program						Season for Use				Location		Ease of Growth (1 = most difficult)	Comments and Special Features
	Annual	Perennial	Biennial	Plant Propagation	Floral Art	Terrariums	Forcing	Garden Design Features	Craft Projects	Spring	Summer	Fall	Winter	Indoor Plants	Outdoor Plants		
Wood fern or marginal shield fern *Dryopteris marginalis*		•		•	•	•			•					•	•	2	Small plants useful in temperate woodland terrariums; fronds useful in floral art; easy to obtain in "meaningful walks."
Geranium *Pelargonium x hortorum*	•			•	•			•		•	•	•	•	•	•	3	Another essential plant; easy to root; most, if not all, patients are familiar with this plant; tolerant of drought.
Bishop's goutweed *Aegopodium podagraria*		•		•				•			•				•	3	Appealing name; vigorous; striking contrast; invasive; good for plant sales.
Hollyhock *Althaea rosea*			•	•	•			•			•				•	3	Old-fashioned; memory stimulating; hardy.
Hoya or wax plant *Hoya carnosa*	•	•		•								•		•		3	Another "action plant" — new growth moves and stretches to follow the light.
Common hyacinth *Hyacinthus orientalis*		b			•		•	•		•		•	•	•	•	3	Pungent, sweet fragrance stimulates conversation and memory; good for forcing, indoor fall projects; forced bulbs are a beautiful surprise in early spring.
English ivy *Hedera helix*		•		•	•	•			•		•			•	•	3	Easily rooted; prefers shade; useful in topiary.

Plant Material Scientific/Common name	Type (w = woody, b = bulb)			Use in Your Hort Therapy Program						Season for Use				Location		Ease of Growth (1 = most difficult)	Comments and Special Features
	Annual	Perennial	Biennial	Plant Propagation	Floral Art	Terrariums	Forcing	Garden Design Features	Craft Projects	Spring	Summer	Fall	Winter	Indoor Plants	Outdoor Plants		
Swedish ivy *Plectranthus oertendahlii*		•		•	•	•				•				•		3	One of the most important in your selection of plant materials; extremely tolerant; loves to be cut back; spikes of waxy, cream-coloured flowers.
English lavender *Lavandula angustifolia*		•		•				•	•		•			•	•	2	Dried leaves and flowers for potpourri; fragrant; musical memories "Lavender Blue."
Fragrant plantain lily *Hosta plantaginea*		•		•	•			•			•	•			•	2	Beautiful contrast as groundcover plant; aroma of creamy white flowers is heavenly.
Nerve plant *Fittonia verschaffeltii argyroneura*	•			•		•				•	•			•		1	Visually attractive due to its unique venation; miniature version is highly useful in terrarium construction.
Easter orchid *Cattleya labiata*		•		•	•								•	•		1	A challenge to propagate and grow; important as a way to mark the celebration of Easter.
Red osier dogwood *Cornus sericea*		w		•	•		•	•	•	•	•				•	3	Very hardy; excellent winter colour; suckers can be gathered and woven for baskets; easy rooting has advantage for positive success rate.
Panda plant *Kalanchoe tomentosa*		•		•				•		•	•			•		2	Effective for their tactile appeal; grow on dry side, making them useful if neglect is a problem.

Plant Material Scientific/Common name	Type (w = woody, b = bulb)			Use in Your Hort Therapy Program						Season for Use				Location		Ease of Growth (1 = most difficult)	Comments and Special Features
	Annual	Perennial	Biennial	Plant Propagation	Floral Art	Terrariums	Forcing	Garden Design Features	Craft Projects	Spring	Summer	Fall	Winter	Indoor Plants	Outdoor Plants		
Flowering quince *Chaenomeles speciosa*		w		•			•	•	•	•	•				•	2	Delicate flowers are among the most beautiful; may be forced indoors; fruit can be made into jelly.
Rainbow inch plant *Tradescantia albiflora* 'Lackensis' (also called *Zebrina*)		•		•	•	•				•				•		3	Useful in hanging baskets as scent plant; very easy to root; useful to grow indoors.
Chinese rose or Chinese hibiscus *Hibiscus rosa-sinensis*		•	•	•	•			•		•	•	•	•			2	Tolerates full sun; spectacular flowers; easy to propagate from cuttings.
Rugosa rose *Rosa rugosa*		w		•	•			•	•	•	•	•			•	2	A species rose; very hardy; old-fashioned; large rose hips in autumn useful in jellies, tea, wreaths.
Pineapple sage *Salvia elegans*		•		•	•					•	•			•	•	1	Must be started from cuttings; difficult to transplant; novelty herb; pineapple-scented oil from leaves; bright scarlet blooms.
Service berry or saskatoon *Amelanchier alnifolia*		w			•		•	•	•	•	•				•	3	Edible berries attract birds; excellent fall colour; manageable height to 3 m (10 ft). Forced in early spring.
Sensitive plant *Mimosa pudica*	•			•		•				•			•	•		1	Another "action plant"; very sensitive to touch (caution: too much touching could weaken plant); easy to grow from seed; a must for your program.

PEOPLE, PLANTS & PROGRAMS   61

Plant Material Scientific/Common name	Type (w = woody, b = bulb)			Use in Your Hort Therapy Program						Season for Use				Location		Ease of Growth (1 = most difficult)	Comments and Special Features
	Annual	Perennial	Biennial	Plant Propagation	Floral Art	Terrariums	Forcing	Garden Design Features	Craft Projects	Spring	Summer	Fall	Winter	Indoor Plants	Outdoor Plants		
Spider plant *Chlorophytum commosum* 'Variegatum'		•		•		•				•	•			•		3	Ease of propagation, habit of growth, name of plant, and adaptability to environment make it a must for an institutional indoor garden.
Venus fly trap *Dionaea muscipula*		•				•			•					•		2	"Action plant" sparks interest; can actually feed plant; ideal for terrariums.
Virgin's bower *Clematis ligusticifolia*	w			•				•			•				•	2	Flowers are dramatic; seed pods are unusual.
Contorted willow *Salix matsudana* 'Tortuosa'	w			•	•		•	•	•	•			•		•	3	Special children's attraction; soft, fur-like flowers; branches contort for analogy and arranging.
Pussy willow *Salix discolor*	w			•	•		•	•	•	•			•		•	3	Willows are extremely useful in horticulture therapy; for analogy.
Wintercreeper *Euonymus fortunei*	w			•	•			•			•	•			•	2	Visually effective; bright red autumn colour; colourful berries and tactile bark; "winged" modification useful to touch for visually impaired.

Table 9
Examples of Common Plants that Dramatically Stimulate Our Senses

Common Name and Latin Name	Setting		Type	Sense Affected				
	Indoor	Outdoor		Sight	Taste	Touch	Hearing	Smell
Aspen *Populus tremuloides*	•	•	tree	•			•	
Basil *Ocimum basilicum*	•	•	herb		•			•
Christmas cactus *Schlumbergera truncata*	•		house plant	•				
Eastern white cedar *Thuja occidentalis*		•	tree/shrub	•		•		•
Delphinium *Delphium elatum*		•	perennial	•				
Hollyhock *Althaea rosea*		•	biennial	•				
Lilac *Syringa* spp.		•	shrub	•				•
Easter lily *Lilium longiflorum*	•		bulb	•				•
Narcissus *Narcissus* spp.	•	•	bulb (forced)	•				•
Snapweed *Impatiens capensis*		•	hardy annual			•	•	

Table 10
Atrium Plants that Stimulate

Plant	Characteristics	Effectiveness	Source
Amaryllis *Hippeastrum* hybrids	Flamboyant, striking, draws attention	Conversation piece; large range of cultivars and colours; stimulates competitive spirit (e.g., who can produce most blooms).	Most garden centres and department stores carry bulbs in August/September
Boston fern *Nephrolepsis exaltata* 'Bostoniensis'	Tranquil, elegant, cool colours	Provides a soothing atmosphere; calming effect; tolerates cooler environment.	Nursery or garden centre
Bromeliads (examples follow)	Exotic, mysterious, outlandish	Cuplike reservoir; stimulates interest and curiosity; flat, spear-like flower stimulates questions.	Garden centre
Pineapple *Ananas comosus*	Edible fruit with exciting taste	Evokes curiosity; can be propagated in a number of ways.	Garden centre, grocery store
Mosaic vase *Guzmania musaica*	Carnivorous plant with coloured bands on leaf	Observe insects in pool of water.	Garden centre
Dracaena *Dracaena marginata*	Dramatic movement, exciting, captures the imagination	Rewarding to grow because easily propagates from stem cuttings; two plants framing a doorway can help orient patient.	Garden centre
Peace lily, white sails *Spathiphyllum wallisii*	Elegant, stately, with pure white flowers. This plant has been designated as important in air purification.	Rewarding to grow because easily started from root division; useful as analogy because does well in low light and can tolerate neglect.	Garden centre

and successes. Adults can also learn a great deal from analogies. Some useful analogies follow.

- Every flower has an environment where it does best; you are like a flower.

- Life began in a garden.

- Weeding a garden helps eliminate many of life's little problems.

- Wisdom, like the oak tree, is slow to mature.

- Plants, like people, can turn out fine, despite adversity.

- There are similarities between plant and human propagation.

- Insects, mites, and diseases — like people — compete for space.

- Contorted branches, like contorted bodies, need not be ugly.

- When growth stops, decay begins.

- Like young trees growing out of old stumps, death can support new life.

- Like searching for blackberries among the thorns, you may have to endure pain in order to experience pleasure.

- If plants are overwatered, overfertilized, or overexposed to light, they can weaken and die; substance abusers are like these plants.

- Annual flowers are at their height of beauty as they approach death due to impending frost.

- Consider the weeping willow: There is beauty in weeping. It is okay to cry, since it can relieve tension and stress and may be cathartic.

There are literally hundreds of such analogies from every discipline (see also Table 11). Many of your older clients may be able to help you create analogies with other old garden proverbs.

Horticulture Knows No Boundaries

Horticulture can be applied to many areas in life. For example, you can blend your clients' other interests — in pets, music, art, etc. — with horticulture to achieve optimum response. For example, clients who enjoy pets can raise vegetables, save vegetable scraps, or harvest dandelions to feed their guinea pigs, or perhaps grow catnip for their cats. These simple activities that blend pet care with gardening give purpose and pleasure to both activities, thereby instilling responsibility and self-esteem in your clients.

There are many other possibilities. Use Table 11 to broaden your own perspective on horticulture and to kindle your clients' imaginations. For instance, involve clients in

Table 11
Ideas to Broaden Horticultural Activities

History	Literature	Music	Art	Geography
History of horticulture from ancient times to early settlers Origin of common economic plants Trade in food and plants	Flowers of Shakespeare Flowers of the Bible	Tchaikovsky's *Waltz of the Flowers*	Famous paintings of gardens, flowers, fruits, and vegetables	Plants of different climates and soils State or provincial flowers and trees

Anthropology	Chemistry	Mathematics	Biology	Languages
Ethnic gardens and use of plants by other cultures Mythology relating to plants	Plant enzymes, photosynthesis, starch test	Symmetrical composition, number of seeds, plant parts, weight of fruits, harvest quality	Botany Evolution of plants Classification of plants	Latin names Names in other languages Etymology or origin of English names

Medicine	Space Exploration	Architecture	Sports	Geology
Herbs and medicinal plants	Tests on plants in space Effects of gravity on plants	Natural influences of plants on architectural styles	Lawn bowling Horse racing (wreath, roses)	Plants and soil formation Plant fossils

Table 12
Activities for Different Months of the Year

	Activity	Value	J	F	M	A	M	J	J	A	S	O	N	D
Active	Moving plants in the greenhouse	Physical exercise, organization	•	•	•	•	•				•	•	•	•
	Carrying pots to be washed	Exercise, gratifying	•	•	•							•	•	•
	Watering flats of plants	Exercise, selective response	•	•	•	•	•	•	•	•	•	•	•	•
	Removing dead leaves	Hand-eye co-ordination, dexterity	•	•	•	•	•	•	•	•	•	•	•	•
	Weeding the garden	Selective response, satisfying				•	•	•	•	•	•	•		
	Taking cuttings	Precision, decision-making, organization	•	•	•		•	•	•	•	•	•		•
	Spading the garden	Exercise, repetition				•	•	•			•	•	•	
	Planting seeds	Co-ordination, precision	•	•	•	•	•	•	•	•	•	•		•
	Hoeing the garden	Exercise, rhythmic activity				•	•	•	•	•	•	•		
	Pushing the wheelbarrow	Exercise				•	•	•	•	•	•	•		
	Harvesting	Fun, physically satisfying							•	•	•	•	•	
Passive	Reading seed catalogues and books on gardening	Learning, planning, remembering	•	•	•	•	•	•	•	•	•	•	•	•
	Watching and identifying birds at feeder	Fascinating, relaxing, learning	•	•	•	•						•	•	•
	Discussing plans for garden projects	Socializing, responsibility	•	•	•	•	•	•	•	•	•	•	•	•
	Tasting fresh fruit and vegetables	Nutritional, stimulating, satisfying					•	•	•	•	•	•	•	
	Smelling herbs and flowers	Satisfying, stimulates memory	•	•	•	•	•	•	•	•	•	•	•	•
	Listening to water, wind, rain	Relaxing, refreshing	•	•	•	•	•	•	•	•	•	•	•	•
	Feeling warmth from sun or cool breeze	Relaxing, comforting	•	•	•	•	•	•	•	•	•	•	•	•
Creative	Choosing right plants for landscape	Decision-making, satisfying	•		•	•	•	•	•	•	•	•	•	•
	Cutting hedges (topiary)	Precision, rewarding				•	•							
	Arranging flowers, foliage	Precision, rewarding				•	•	•	•	•	•	•	•	
	Cooking foods from garden	Nutritional, fun, gratifying	•	•	•	•	•	•	•	•	•	•	•	•
	Weaving wreaths, baskets	Original, rewarding, useful, co-ordination				•	•	•	•	•	•	•	•	
	Pruning shrubs, flowers, trees; tying and training vines, fruit trees, etc.	Precision, physical exercise, useful		•	•	•	•				•	•		
	Exhibiting flowers, vegetables	Competition, excitement, rewarding							•	•	•			
	Decorating home for festive occasion	Originality, useful	•	•	•	•	•	•	•	•	•	•	•	•

Table 13
Fall and Winter Garden Activities

Autumn	Winter
Going on walks to collect berries, nuts, grasses	Collecting winter wood, bird watching, photography
Planting bulbs	Visiting local greenhouses to see what activities are going on in winter (forced bulbs, poinsettias)
Digging root crops	Visiting the farmers' market
Canning and preserving fruits and vegetables, drying herbs	Gift making
Preparing the garden for winter: raking, mulching, bundling garden stalks, cleaning and storing tools	Looking for signs of spring in warm, sheltered areas
	Forcing branches of apple, cherry, dogwood in late winter

a dice game where simple questions relating to plants — favourite flowers, favourite foods, people named after flowers — could be answered. This would involve group participation and stimulate discussion. Another idea might be to have your clients co-operate to produce a horticultural "Trivial Pursuit." They could research different aspects and develop appropriate questions, create the rules, and design the board and the tokens. They could make multiple copies of the game to give as gifts to friends and relatives.

Horticultural Activities All Year Long

For thousands of people, gardening is a way of life all year long. Following the seasons, planning next year's garden, ordering seeds, starting plants indoors, seeding, cultivating,

and harvesting can all be meaningful, pleasurable experiences. And there are many other possibilities for activities throughout the year. A comfortable blend of active, passive, and creative activities in each session and in your overall program will help maintain client interest. Table 12 gives ideas for activities for different months of the year. Planning fall and winter outdoor activities may take a bit more imagination, but it is worth it. Table 13 has a few more ideas to get you started in fall and winter activities.

This chapter described how to select plants for your program, use plants as analogies, and increase the social benefits of gardening. It provided examples of programs. The following chapter will take you through a step-by-step approach to setting up your own horticulture therapy program.

Chapter 6

⊰━◈━◦━◈━⊱

Starting a Horticulture Therapy Program

Ahorticulture therapy program involves setting goals, developing objectives based on those goals, setting up activities that will meet those objectives, implementing the activities, and evaluating their results. But where do you start?

Setting Goals

You need to know what you want to accomplish in your horticulture therapy program. The best way to do this is to sit down and define your long-term goals. A goal is a destination, like the point where a race ends. Your goal might be to improve the physical, emotional, social, and spiritual outlook of your clients through horticulture. For example, you may want to focus on enhancing the horticultural aspects of your space so that it will benefit your clients. To develop your goals, assess the capabilities of your clients and discuss their needs and desires with them.

Many hospitals and institutions receive only general cosmetic landscape treatment, and often little is done to enhance their interiors. You will likely need to create or modify garden areas for use in your program. Before any modifications are made, consult with your clients, a landscape architect or designer, medical and paramedical personnel, and the institution's administration. Everyone should have a complete understanding of the program's objectives and goals, the changes that will be made, and how the area will be used and maintained. Remember as well that the general public is influenced by these changes, which ultimately could benefit your program if the setting is used regularly. For example, a nicely landscaped area with picnic tables will attract staff, family, and friends. When your clients see other people socializing, they, in turn, will feel less isolated.

The cost of developing a therapeutic garden area should be separate from general grounds or indoor maintenance. If administrators at your institution agree that the therapeutic value of these areas should be developed for patients, staff, and visitors, then you have a strong case for financial assistance to develop and maintain them.

There are hundreds of excellent reference books, pamphlets, magazine and newspaper articles, as well as extension courses to help you with indoor and outdoor garden design. Some of these are listed in the Resources chapter. Chapters 2 and 3 provide more information and ideas on modifications to make these areas more enjoyable and more therapeutically valuable for your clients.

Before you set your goals, you will probably want to spend some time thinking about horticulture and horticulture therapy. Here are some tips to start you off.

- Talk to other therapists in your own or other institutions about horticulture therapy. They may already be using it or know of someone who is.

- Think about how a horticulture program could fit in with other therapeutic activities to meet your clients' needs while making the best use of available resources. You may need to reduce, modify, or eliminate some activities to give horticulture priority, or you may find innovative ways to blend horticulture with other programs.

- Call horticultural societies, garden clubs, Master Gardeners, horticulture extension services, local garden centres, nurseries, parks departments, and volunteer agencies for volunteer gardeners to help with the development or implementation of the program. Ask your clients if they know any avid gardeners who might be able to help.

- Take stock of the facilities, supplies, and plant materials already available to you. Think about additional items you might need and find out where you could beg, borrow, or buy them.

- Think about which clients would benefit from the program. Limit the size of your group. (See Chapter 5 for more details.) As noted earlier, there should be a 1:2 ratio of volunteers and staff to clients. If there are too many clients, individuals will not receive enough attention, and the activity area will become confusing and distracting.

- Start to assemble a library of resources and reference materials. You may wish to ask an interested client or volunteer to collect the information and enter a bibliography on a computer disk for easy reference.

While developing your program, remember to KISS — Keep It Short and Simple. Often when we get excited about something new or special we want to learn, try, do, and reap all we can from it — all at once. There is nothing wrong with learning, trying, and doing, as long as your expectations are reasonable and manageable.

Setting Objectives

Each activity in your program should be designed to meet certain therapeutic objectives, that is, to produce a certain response from your clients. The objectives should help to accomplish the overall goal of your horticulture therapy program. For example, the goal of your program might be to improve the physical and emotional outlooks of your clients, while an objective of an activity might be to improve your clients' motor co-ordination and increase their patience through propagating herbs in window boxes.

A basic objective of every activity must be enjoyment. To enjoy something, we must be interested in it. Interest produces motivation, and motivation produces participation and enjoyment. One of horticulture's most valuable characteristics is that it provides interest, motivation, participation, and enjoyment for many people, regardless of age, gender, or background. In addition to enjoyment, the activities will have other specific physical and/or psychological objectives (like increasing hand-eye co-ordination or promoting decision-making) based on the needs and capabilities of your clients.

For horticulture therapy to be effective, there has to be a partnership between clients, therapist, volunteers, and anyone else concerned with the outcome of the therapy. Develop objectives through discussions with these people. In particular, client participation in setting objectives will increase the likelihood of meeting the objectives. As you get to know your clients' interests, try to find ways to blend their interests with horticulture to give greater purpose and pleasure to the activities.

Figure 15 illustrates how therapeutic objectives can be met using a step-by-step approach. This format is applicable to any gardening activity. Completed charts can be used as an inventory of activities with proven benefits.

This diagram describes three horticultural

Figure 15. Meeting Therapeutic Objectives

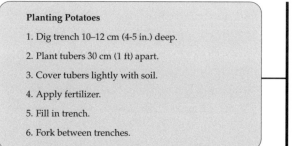

Planting Potatoes

1. Dig trench 10–12 cm (4-5 in.) deep.

2. Plant tubers 30 cm (1 ft) apart.

3. Cover tubers lightly with soil.

4. Apply fertilizer.

5. Fill in trench.

6. Fork between trenches.

Objectives

e.g., performing tasks in sequence

-
-
-
-
-
-

Harvesting Onions

1. Bend tops over to hasten ripening.

2. Lift onions with roots facing sun.

3. Lay crop on wire frame in cool, well-ventilated area to dry.

4. Make onion rope by tying onions onto dry stalk sheaf.

5. Hang finished rope in cool, dry area.

6. Cut onions from rope as needed.

Objectives

-
-
-
-
-
-

Preparing a Seed Bed

1. Firm cultivated ground.

2. Rake to obtain fine texture.

3. Set out rows using metre stick.

4. Draw rows for seed.

5. Sow seed.

6. Cover seed and rake over seed bed.

Objectives

-
-
-
-
-
-

activities: 1) planting potatoes, 2) harvesting onions, or 3) preparing a seed bed. Opposite the steps given under each activity, list possible therapeutic objectives.

Besides the specific therapeutic objectives of performing a task, there may be many more objectives that are taken for granted, are forgotten, or go unnoticed, e.g., movement/relocation from one environment to another (indoors/outdoors), or the nutritional value of growing the residents'/clients' own vegetables. You may want to list these routine objectives in your step-by-step plan as a reminder to yourself and to help you in developing a well-rounded approach in your program.

Selecting a Site

Use a team approach when choosing your site. Administrators, groundskeepers or maintenance staff, other caregivers, volunteers, and, most important, your clients should all have an opportunity for input.

Programs can take place indoors, outdoors, or in a greenhouse. An indoor location is usually the most convenient and least expensive for those just beginning, and novice gardeners may find it less threatening. (Choosing sites for outdoor and indoor activities is described in Chapters 2 and 3.) Remember that the work area must be easily accessible. It should have sufficient space to comfortably accommodate plants, materials, and your clients (who may be in wheelchairs, or need walkers), perhaps including extra space in late winter and early spring for seedlings, transplants, and potted bedding plants. It should be bright and cheery, but strong direct sunlight should be avoided, particularly if you are working with seniors or people on medication that makes them sensitive to light.

For indoor gardening, horticulture activities need not be confined to the activity area. Small plants can be taken to clients' rooms. The point is to have a place set aside as a focal point for your horticulture activities — a place to propagate and grow plants, to store materials, and to show others how horticulture therapy works.

Although a greenhouse has many advantages (see Chapter 2), remember that its atmosphere is not usually conducive to both plants and clients. High temperatures, noise from fans, vents, and misting systems, and other factors may make it a less-than-ideal work area. If possible, have a separate, comfortable work area for your clients that is as close to the greenhouse as possible.

The great outdoors also has advantages, but be prepared for many distractions, unexpected visitors (good and not so good), insect pests, and, of course, bad weather. Safety is also a concern (see Chapter 7 for appropriate safety measures). An outdoor site should be carefully selected to ensure that it is suitable for plants and for people (see Chapter 3).

Planning and Implementing Activities

Your first horticulture therapy activities should be as simple as possible. Many basic ideas in children's gardening books are extremely useful when working with clients with cognitive impairment and physical limitations.

Start small with a few pots, some soil, seeds, and water, and then watch how things grow! The following tips will help each activity go smoothly and meet its objectives.

- Before the activity, work out the time needed for each step. Be sure to allow time for set up, your instructions and explanations, clients' questions, unexpected difficulties, and cleaning up. Have a clear understanding of what participants might learn from the activities you have planned.

- Arrive early to set up. Make sure the tables are in a comfortable arrangement; circular or U-shaped is usually preferable.

- Have more than enough materials, just in case someone arrives unexpectedly.

- Give proper introductions and wrap-ups to the activity.

- Involve your clients as much as possible in all stages of the activity.

- Keep the objectives of the activity in mind at all times, but be flexible to change and interruptions.

- Do not overwork one method of teaching. A mixture of visuals, hands-on activities, rest periods, and time to reflect are essential to the success of your gardening activity.

Figure 16 illustrates how you can set up a lesson plan to record the activity, the participants, what was done and how it was done, materials and teaching aids used, and the results. Before long, you will have a book full of your lesson plans for a variety of horticultural activities. You will find this invaluable for assessing the progress of your clients and fine-tuning your program. It will also be a great help for the therapists who follow you.

Materials and Supplies

Materials and supplies need not be elaborate or expensive. In fact, some of the most effective programs (e.g., Japanese flower arranging) focus on the basics and purposely keep materials to a minimum. (Chapters 2 and 3 describe many of the items you may wish to use, and Chapter 4 provides ideas

Figure 16. Simple Lesson Plan

Objective:	Topic: Herb gardening	Date/Time: Jan. 21, 1994
To learn how to propagate herbs for use in hospital window boxes.	Instructor(s): Ms. Brown	Room: Rec 101
	Participants: Mr. Smith, Mrs. Davies, Mrs. Allen, Mr. Jones, Ms. Keer	

Instructional Techniques:

Ask if anyone has done this before. Show pictures of herbs and demonstrate planting techniques. Have volunteers help prepare soil mix, labels, and seed.

Time	Instructor's Activities	Participants' Activities	Supplies
5 min	Demonstrating step-by-step seeding methods.	Mixing soil. Filling pots with soil.	Soil Pots Variety of herb seeds
20 min	Assisting volunteers and partici-pants with soil, seeds, pots, and labels. Mixing fine seed with sand.	Identifying their seeds. Writing out labels and sowing seed in their pots. Watering pots. Placing pots in light garden.	Slides/pictures of herbs Projector Books, catalogues Watering can Aprons for laps Sand
5 min	Assisting participants in clean-up and answering any questions they may have.	Helping clean-up and arranging pots.	
Total: 30 min			

Comments:

Mr. Smith had problems sorting out seeds.

Mrs. Allen helped Mr. Jones.

More time should have been left for clean-up.

for inexpensive tools and equipment.)

The diagrammatic checklist of greenhouse materials and supplies (Figure 17) is a useful tool with which to begin a program.

Budgeting

Horticulture is probably the most economical form of therapy there is. It is all around us and much is free. And with an imaginative approach, there's no limit to what you can do.

Table 14 is a suggested budget for the set-up costs of a modest indoor gardening program. (Counter space, sinks, tables, and specialized tools and equipment have not been included. These items will be part of the overall resources of your facility and will vary within each institution.) Prices are only approximate and reflect the needs of a group of 15 people over a one-year period.

Remember that costs can be reduced in a number of ways. Wholesale rates are often available to institutions or individuals having accounts with suppliers. Talk with local wholesale and retail suppliers and tell them about your program, its objectives, and its clients. They may be willing to donate old stock items or sell them at reduced rates. Some may provide plants, tools, or equipment for advertising and promotion privileges. The possibilities are endless for mutual co-operation and volunteer assistance and support between you and the horticultural industry.

Scheduling People/Plant Activities

The quality of life of both people and plants is enhanced through effective scheduling. Scheduling with plant life cycles in mind facilitates client response. Effective scheduling will improve the quality of your program and strengthen its credibility:

- Scheduling provides an accurate record of the sequence of events throughout the year which can be modified as the needs of your program change and develop.

- Planning can begin a year in advance once you are familiar with the dates of such activities as seeding, bulb planting, forcing, and pruning.

- Scheduling will help you keep track of what should be happening in the next few months, giving you more time to organize client participation and staff and volunteer assistance, and to order materials and supplies. As a result, your program will become better organized and more professional.

Many gardening books, magazines, and government publications and fact sheets have detailed information on scheduling of horticultural activities. (See Resource chapter for more information.)

Plants follow a natural sequence of events in their life cycles. For most indoor and outdoor plants, fall and winter are times of

Figure 17
Materials and Supplies Organized on the Potting Bench

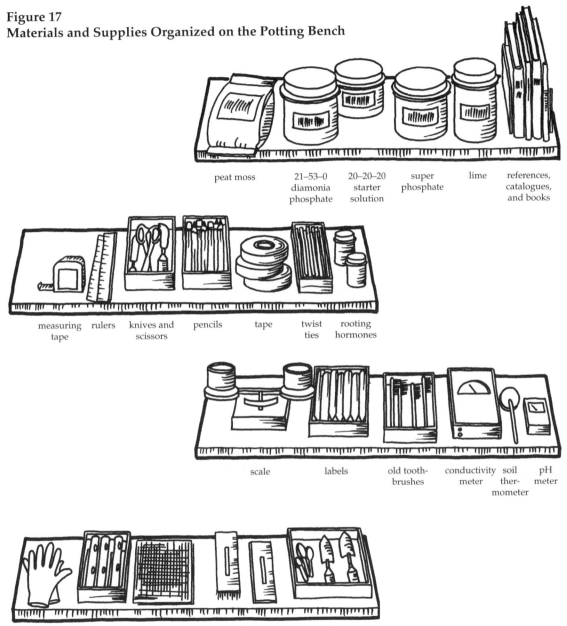

peat moss   21–53–0   20–20–20   super   lime   references,
               diamonia   starter   phosphate   catalogues,
               phosphate   solution   and books

measuring rulers knives and   pencils   tape   twist   rooting
tape   scissors   ties   hormones

scale   labels   old tooth-   conductivity soil   pH
                             brushes   meter   ther-   meter
                                                         mometer

rubber gloves   dibblers   screens   brushes   measuring spoons,
                                                  trowels

Table 14. Example of a Materials and Supplies Budget

Item	Quantity	Description	Price (approx, excl. tax) Unit ($)	Total ($)
Equipment				
Storage bins	3	Plastic, 225 litre (50 gal/59 US gal) capacity	15.00	45.00
Propagation mat	1	Heating cables for propagation bench		50.00
Thermometer	1	Air		6.00
Watering can	2	2 litre (4 pint/2 qt) plastic	15.00	30.00
Pails	2	5 litre (10 pint/5 qt) plastic	7.00	14.00
Supplies				
Peat pellets	1,000	Regular and predrilled holes for cuttings		75.00
Pots: plastic and clay types	200 200 100	Assorted 7.6 cm (3 in.) Assorted 12.7cm (5 in.) Assorted 20 cm (10 in.)		30.00 30.00 30.00
Flats	500	Cell packs, assorted sizes		60.00
Labels: (plastic or wooden)	500	12.5 cm (5 in.) indoor labelling and 20 cm (8 in.) outdoor labelling		30.00
Markers, waterproof	2	Maybe 4 or 6, depending on group size	7.00	14.00
Soils: peat moss perlite vermiculite	10 10 10	Refined horticultural 0.1 cu m (4 cu ft) Horticultural grade 0.1 cu m (4 cu ft) Horticultural grade 0.1 cu m (4 cu ft)	12.00 10.00 10.00	120.00 100.00 100.00
Rooting hormone	2	#1 and #2 for softwood cuttings	8.00	16.00
Tools				
Shovel	1	Lightweight aluminum		12.00
Trowels Propagating knives	15 5	Lightweight wood handle Ratchet type, if available	8.00 15.00	120.00 75.00
Broom Wisk Dust Pan	1	Corn, lightweight	7.00	7.00
Pesticides				
Insecticidal soaps	1 case	1 litre (1 qt) spray bottles		30.00
Fungicides				45.00
Total				1039.00

rest (dormancy), while the spring and summer months are active growing periods. Within these two main periods, plants go through various stages of development. The schedule of your clients' gardening activities should be based on plant life cycles.

Plants can also be used as timepieces to indicate when to carry out gardening activities. For example, when lilac leaves are 3 cm (1 in.) long, you can plant corn. This earlier planting will help to reduce crop damage by the corn borer. Some people also plant by phase of the moon. They would advise that flowering lilac, corn, and peas should be planted at full moon, and root crops such as carrots and beets are planted with no moon. While such folklore is interesting, research does not substantiate it all.

The following is an example of the sequence of bloom of flowers which provides colour, interest, and client involvement in the outdoor garden from early spring to late fall.

Early spring: Bulbs such as grape hyacinth, narcissus, and tulip.

Spring: Pansies, violas, spring adonis, clematis, and rose daphne.

Summer: Annuals such as calendula, cosmos, and cleome; perennials like delphinium, ligularia, and monkshood; roses and lilies, which provide height and colour until early autumn.

Autumn: Perennials such as chrysanthemums, blanketflower, and fall asters.

Late autumn: The flowers of the autumn crocus herald the onset of winter.

Table 15 will give you some ideas for people/plant activities throughout the year. The activities described should be fleshed out with further information from gardening books, periodicals, and other publications to make the activities practical for your work setting and to suit the capabilities of your clients.

> To every thing there is a season, and a time to every purpose under the heaven:
>
> A time to be born, and a time to die; a time to plant, and a time to pluck up that which is planted;
>
> A time to kill, and a time to heal; a time to break down, and a time to build up;
>
> A time to weep, and a time to laugh; a time to mourn, and a time to dance;
>
> A time to cast away stones, and a time to gather stones together; a time to embrace, and a time to refrain from embracing;
>
> A time to get, and a time to lose; a time to keep, and a time to cast away;
>
> A time to rend, and a time to sew; a time to keep silence, and a time to speak;
>
> A time to love, and a time to hate; a time of war, and a time of peace.
>
> *Ecclesiastes 3: 1–8*

Table 15. Scheduling People/Plant Activities

Month	Indoor	Outdoor	Greenhouse
January	• Make cuttings from indoor plants. • Show films and slides of last year's garden and famous gardens. • Order seeds from garden catalogues. • Inspect bulbs in cold storage. • Clean up, repair, and take inventory of garden tools.	• Stock bird feeders.	• Start cuttings in propagation bench. • Review steps in seed sowing.
February	• Make terrariums and hanging baskets from cuttings started in January. • Begin forcing spring bulbs in cold storage. • Seed sowing. • Flower arrangements for Valentine's Day.	• Prune flowering shrubs for indoor forcing. • Check bird feeder; add some gravel to mix. • Check trees and shrubs for deer and rabbit damage.	• Take cuttings from healthy stock plants. • Start some summer bulbs (e.g., gladioli) early for forcing. • Do germination test on last year's seed.
March	• Air layer plants such as dieffenbachia and fig. • Transplant seedlings in "true leaf" stage from seed sown in February. • Excellent month for repotting old house plants.	• Start dormant pruning. • Apply dormant oil spray to fruit trees.	• Watch for overwatering and poor air circulation causing damping off. • Start tender vegetables (tomatoes, cucumbers). • Repot house plants. • Increase shelf space in order to make room for transplants from seed flats.
April	• Make a chart identifying the different vegetable seeds. • Easter flower arranging. • Visit conservatory or greenhouse.	• Start "working" your cold frames, and "hardening" your seedling transplants. • Prepare garden area and flower beds when soil is sufficiently dry. • In late April, sow cool-weather crops like cabbage, lettuce, sweet peas. • Raking and general clean-up. • Prune tea roses.	• Run at cooler temperature to help keep bedding plants compact by slowing down growth. • Provide shading from intensity of sun.
May	• Start planning for fall activities such as collecting flowers for pressing. • Start cuttings from begonia and African violets. • Mother's Day plant sale.	• Plant summer bulbs (gladioli, dahlias) and move most bedding plants to cold frames or directly to garden. • "Direct" sowing of perennial seeds, warm-season vegetables, and planting hardened transplants (broccoli, tomato, corn). Note: "Hot caps" may be needed over tomatoes, cucumber, and corn in northern areas.	• Wash down glass, floors, and benches. • Plan for fall and winter crops. • Organize supplies, shelves.
June	• Fresh flower arranging. • Prepare hummingbird feeders to set out on patio.	• Succession cropping (lettuce, beans, corn, etc.). • Identify and label all flowering trees and shrubs. • Tie up leaves of spring flowering bulbs (do not remove foliage) and plant annual bedding plants around them. • Mulch between rows in garden.	• Take cuttings from such plants as chrysanthemum, poinsettia, and bougainvillea. • Wash leaves of large house plants and watch for insect pests (scale, white fly, and aphid).

Month	Indoor	Outdoor	Greenhouse
July	• Try to do all craft-like activities out of doors on patio or in sheltered area.	• Turn compost pile. • Cultivate, weed, and water garden. • Start harvesting herbs and early vegetables (peas, beans, onions). • Prune evergreens and deciduous hedges. • Harvest "everlastings" for winter flower arranging.	• Plant rooted poinsettia and chrysan-themum cuttings. • Order bulbs for fall planting.
August	• Drying herbs	• Arrange for local garden tour. • Divide garden perennials (e.g., iris). • Remove old fruiting canes from raspberries. • All aspects of harvesting.	• Take cuttings from poinsettia stock plants.
September	• Plan a Fall Fair. • Do dried flower arrangements. • Pot up bulbs for forcing.	• Sow winter rye in garden as green manure crop. • Deadhead bedding plants. • Plant spring flowering bulbs (tulips, crocus, narcissus).	• Watch for excessive humidity build-up providing ideal conditions for diseases such as mildew and botrytis.
October	• Make Thanksgiving centrepiece for dining room. • Carve pumpkins. • Prepare vegetable root crops for storage.	• Dig dahlias and gladioli and rake and compost leaves. • Plant cold-hardy annual seed such as larkspur, calliopsis, calendula, and snapdragon for early spring. • Cut sunflower seed heads and air dry indoors away from birds and squirrels.	• Poinsettias are forming flower buds. Take care that they are not exposed to artificial light.
November	• Use pressed flowers collected and prepared in spring and summer to make cards and gifts. • Make winter bouquets using dried materials grown in your garden or collected on walks.	• Wash and take in outdoor lawn furniture and accessories (bird baths). • Hill roses. • When ground is frozen, mulch roses and other tender plants.	• Force 'Paper White' narcissus. • Watch for aphid and white fly infestation on mums and poinsettias.
December	• Start forcing amaryllis for February blooms (under lights or in greenhouse). • Make Christmas wreaths, garlands, and swags. • Set out bird feeders. • Review last year's garden plans and make any revisions. • Order seed catalogues.	• Protect fruit trees.	• Reduce watering and refrain from fertilizing during the winter months. • Watering should be done in the morning so the soil surface has a chance to dry before evening.

Use your imagination to develop spin-off activities based on the suggestions in the schedules. For example, vegetable harvests could be followed by a produce weigh-in competition; flowers harvested in August could provide material for dried flower arrangements in the winter; and pine cones collected in June could be used for wreath-making in November. (See Resource chapter.)

For greenhouse programs, develop a production schedule for common greenhouse plants such as poinsettias and Easter lilies. *The Ball Red Book*, edited by Vic Ball of Chicago, is an excellent resource for greenhouse scheduling.

Assessment

Assessment may seem like just more paperwork added to the mountain of paperwork you already have, but it is an essential part of your horticulture therapy program. A volunteer might be able to complete this assessment under supervision. Assessing each task provides an effective way to measure its usefulness and provides the guidance essential for the ongoing development of the program. Assessing the progress of individual clients will help you to fine-tune activities to meet their needs. Evaluating the program as a whole is a good way to determine ways to improve the program and to establish the effectiveness of horticulture therapy.

Task Assessment

Task assessment should be based on a detailed account of the task and the steps in performing it, the person(s) performing it, and the results (positive or negative). The therapist should note how the task was performed, what was needed to do the job, and whether it should be modified, improved, or left as is for future programs. Records of these notations of individual tasks can be kept in the comments section of the lesson plans as shown in Figure 16.

An important consideration in task assessment is the degree of success clients have had in growing plants. If the cutting rooted, the seed germinated, or the forced bulb bloomed on time, your clients will have a sense of accomplishment and pride, vital components of successful therapy.

Client Progress

Client progress over time can be recorded on the type of form shown in Figure 18. In this example, each of the three factors to be evaluated — the client's characteristics, his or her recognition of tools, and his or her task performance — has its own column. The specific characteristics, tools, and tasks to be assessed are listed. You will need to modify the form to fit the factors you are assessing and the tasks being carried out.

Figure 18
Task Assessment Form

Name:							Horticultural Task:							Week Ending:						
Characteristics							**Recognition of Tools**							**Performance of Task**						
	M	T	W	T	F	S		M	T	W	T	F	S		M	T	W	T	F	S
Attendance							Rake							Locating tools						
							Hoe													
Enthusiasm							Spade							Proper use						
							Trowel													
Attitude to supervision							Broom							Returning tools to storage						
							Wisk													
Comprehension and memory							Shovel							Co-ordination						
							Sieve													
Quality of performance							Secateurs							Tidiness						
							Pot													
Time to accomplish task							Fertilizer							Quality of work						
							Lawn mower													
Effort to improve							Garden hose							Comments:						
							Watering can													
Key 1 = low level of competence 2 = shows some competence 3 = fair 4 = acceptable 5 = excellent																				

The key at the bottom of the form provides an easy numerical rating system from 1 (poor) to 5 (excellent).

In general, your system of assessment should be flexible, realistic, and sensitive to the capabilities of your clients. Through careful analysis of each component of a task, you can break down the task into manageable parts. As well, by determining a logical sequence of steps, the success of the activity is ensured.

For each step, try to list the objective, what you would like to measure, and the type of response you are looking for. You might like to use such verbs as "holds," "selects," and "digs" to help you define the objectives. An example is given for each task.

It is important to reinforce each component of a task or objective. When listing the objectives, remember that all of them may not be realized in a given time frame and that in gardening there is usually another opportunity to try to accomplish an objective. The aim should be to see the task to completion rather than to follow some arbitrary timeline.

Program Evaluation

Program evaluation should be carried out on a regular basis to determine how you can improve the program and to demonstrate the effectiveness of horticulture therapy to others. It should involve patients, other staff, and volunteers in a team approach to improve and modify the program. It is often useful to review your task assessment and client evaluation records before evaluating the program as a whole.

This chapter described planning your horticulture therapy program, how to define goals, set objectives, and design simple lesson plans to help organize and record activity. Scheduling people/ plant activities, planning a simple budget, and assessment/evaluation procedures were also discussed. The next chapter deals with the safety aspects of gardening and includes a list of plants that should be recognized for hazardous properties.

Chapter 7

>━━◆━◦━◆━━◄

Safety

Safety in horticulture is just as important as in any other activity involving equipment and influenced by weather and other external factors. It is best to take a preventative approach: be aware of potential hazards from weather, equipment, materials, and plants, and take appropriate measures to reduce the risk of accidents and illness. The following ten areas can be used as a safety checklist for your program.

Exposure

Wear gloves to protect hands against abrasions and foreign matter such as splinters and to prevent blisters while raking, pruning, etc. Wear proper footwear indoors and out to protect the feet against abrasions, burns, and injury from debris or falling tools. Good shoes or boots will also provide support and traction on slippery and uneven surfaces.

Rays from the sun are potentially hazardous. Always wear protective clothing, even on the hottest days, to shield the skin from excessive exposure to sunlight and sunburns. Sunscreens may also be appropriate in some cases, but it is important to ensure that your client is not allergic to them. Wear a comfortable hat with a wide brim to shade the head and neck. Wear sunglasses when working in direct sunlight. Remember that clients on medication are always at risk when working in direct sunlight. Their outdoor activities should take place in filtered light during the cooler times of the day.

Many people are allergic to dust, soil, and plants. If these people are keen to participate in your program, they should be properly protected with face masks or given alternative activities to perform if allergic reactions are suspected.

Be especially careful when mixing dry peat moss and perlite. The dust from these materials is extremely irritating. Always moisten the mixture with water from a hose or watering can before turning it, and wear a respirator while moistening.

Physical Activity

Keep the back as straight and relaxed as possible when bending, standing, lifting, or kneeling. To lift objects, bend the knees slightly and then straighten to an upright position. Whenever possible, slide rather than lift heavy objects. Avoid standing for prolonged periods. When standing, try to distribute your weight evenly on both feet. If support from walkers, canes, or crutches is necessary, select work areas that provide maximum stability.

Avoid overexertion. Reaching, pushing, stretching, and all other activities should be done in moderation. Using common sense will avoid many potential problems.

Pest Control for Plants

If insects, weeds, or diseases cause problems for your plants, assess each problem carefully, consider the possible control measures, and choose the method that will most safely provide adequate control.

Some chemical pesticides are potentially hazardous to beneficial insects, birds, small mammals, or people. The handling, application, and storage of pesticides must be the responsibility of a trained supervisor. Pesticides, no matter how safe they are said to be, should be stored in a locked cupboard with adequate ventilation to the outside. Only pesticides registered for a particular pest and plant should be used.

When considering possible pest control measures, remember that there are many alternatives to hazardous chemical pesticides. Here are a few suggestions.

- Make your own insecticide by adding 30 ml (1 fluid oz) of liquid soap to 1 L (1 quart) of water. Apply this to infested leaves using a watering can or an atomizer.

- All pesticides, regardless of their origin ("chemical" or "biological"), may be potentially harmful to clients if handled improperly. Read the label on the pesticide container carefully and follow all label directions exactly. A good rule of thumb is to allow only the horticultural therapist or a knowledgeable volunteer to handle pesticides. Clients with physical or intellectual impairments should not be given this responsibility. Store all pesticides safely under lock when not in use.

- Reduce pesticide use by planting

varieties of trees, shrubs, flowers, and vines that are relatively disease- and insect-resistant. For example, plant 'Thunderchild' flowering crabapple, which is resistant to fireblight.

- Try seed that has been pretreated to control disease. Be sure to wear gloves when sowing treated seed, and prevent children and others from putting the treated seeds in their mouths.

- Try cultural control of insects. This can be done by interfering with their life cycles. For example: hosing down plants, regular cultivation at appropriate times, and hand picking insects from the plants. (See Publications in Resource chapter.)

- Use an old toothbrush to remove scale insects from stems and leaves.

- Place tar-paper disks around the base of cabbage plants when planting seedlings. This will prevent cabbage flies from laying eggs at the base of the plants in June.

- Rotate crops in vegetable gardens to discourage soil-borne diseases and insects associated with particular plants from attacking those plants year after year.

- Avoid planting such vegetables as onions and other root crops in rows.

Row planting makes it easy for the onion maggot to destroy the crop.

- Try companion planting. That is, mix annual flowers and herbs that naturally repel insects in amongst your garden vegetables. Marigolds and scented geraniums are examples plants that may discourage insects. As well, aroma from onions or garlic will control the carrot fly.

- Cleanliness and good cultural practices are extremely important. Rake up garden debris in the autumn and burn or trash it to get rid of eggs, larvae, pupae, etc., of harmful insects. Do not compost pest-ridden debris!

- If at all possible, avoid using herbicides for weed control. In a small garden, weeds are usually not a problem if good gardening practices like mulching, cultivating, spot weeding, and mowing are carried out on a regular basis. All of these activities are, of course, great for assessing clients' abilities and can provide much satisfaction to clients for a job well done.

Pest Control for People

Certain garden pests can be a nuisance to people. Ants, mosquitoes, wasps, and flies are the most common problems and, if not controlled, can become major irritants in outdoor garden activities.

Start by locating the source of the problem. Scout around for anthills and try to physically discourage the ants by destroying their colonies. Mosquitoes breed in stagnant water, so do not leave water standing in bird baths, wheelbarrows, pails, etc. Flies and wasps are attracted to spoiling animal and vegetable matter. To minimize their activity, burn or compost over-ripe fruit, turn compost frequently, and store organic wastes in a container with a tight-fitting lid. Encourage clients to wear appropriate protective clothing to minimize stings and bites.

Water

People like to play with water. Water is relaxing and fun, but it can pose some problems. Drinking from hoses is not recommended because of the potential for contamination from a variety of materials. If water is spilled, especially on nonporous surfaces that can become slippery, it should be mopped up. Also, remember that people can drown even in shallow water, so use common sense around ponds, pools, and other bodies of water.

Electrical Outlets and Power Equipment

All tools, machinery, and fixtures should be checked regularly to make sure there are no bare wires or faulty plugs or switches. Most plugs today have a ground wire that should comply with government standards. If there is no ground wire, have one installed. Outdoor plugs and lighting receptacles should be waterproof and meet approved standards.

Use extreme caution with power equipment. Power tools, lawn mowers, lawn vacuums, rototillers, and other equipment should be inspected regularly. Operator's manuals should be read and understood before any attempt is made to operate equipment. Deciding who uses which tools must be the responsibility of the therapist. Close supervision of clients and respect for equipment will help prevent accidents. Proper clothing and protection for the eyes, hands, and feet are essential.

Hand Tools and Other Equipment

Since most tools function best when their blades are sharp, decisions as to who works with what tools are crucial. Tools should be put away carefully when not in use so people do not bump into or trip over them. A labeled tool area will facilitate this.

Use caution when working with any support such as bamboo canes, garden stakes, and fencing. It is quite easy to accidentally poke the eyes or face when bending over near stakes. Try colouring the stakes or padding the tips so such accidents will not happen (see Figure 19).

Work Environment

A neat, uncluttered work environment is essential. Tripping on items, slipping on floors, and bumping into things are all less likely to happen if the activity area is kept tidy. For older clients who may be confused, things that are out of place can be distracting

**Figure 19
Safety Hints**

padded stake

large labels

use scissors whenever possible

knife in sheath

and frustrating. Try to have a place for everything, and everything in its place. Label everything for easy identification. (See Figure 17.)

Properly lit sheds, work areas, and patios are also essential to the safety, efficiency, and productivity of your clients.

Garden Paths

Special attention should be paid to safety on garden paths for visually impaired and physically challenged clients. A few simple measures will improve path safety.

- Paths should be a minimum of 1.5 m (5 ft) wide and should provide sufficient turning area for wheelchairs.

- Keep paths clean and free of water and debris.

- Remove algae, moss, or liverworts. In the short term, sprinkle washing soda crystals over them, or use domestic bleach and scrub. Ensure there is no run-off onto lawns or flower beds. You can also use a commercial fungicide or algicide. Follow label directions. Those containing dichlorophen will kill moss. These treatments will need to be repeated unless permanent modifications are made, such as reducing or eliminating shady or poorly ventilated conditions and removing surface moisture which will discourage unwanted growth.

- Make sure the area is well-lit and handrails are present for extra confidence.

- Improve the surface texture of the path to give a better grip. Several methods are available depending on the type of surface (see Chapter 3).

Hazardous and Poisonous Plants

Many common plants can be poisonous or hazardous to some degree. It is the therapist's responsibility to help prevent accidental poisoning. By taking the following steps, you can reduce plant-related accidents in your horticulture therapy activities.

- Learn the names of the plants you are working with, just as you know the names of your clients. Label each plant and include the scientific name in case emergency identification is required.

- Learn to spot poisonous plants. Post a list of common poisonous house plants where your clients can refer to it. Make everyone aware of any poisonous plants in the area. Encourage clients to handle these plants with caution and to wash their hands thoroughly after working with them.

- Be prepared for an emergency. Keep the telephone number of the local poison control centre or hospital handy.

If someone is suspected of ingesting plant material, keep calm, determine how much was eaten, identify the plant, and call the poison control centre. If you are asked to take the individual for an examination, bring some or all of the plant with you.

- Tolerance to plant toxicity varies among individuals; some people will be much more sensitive than others.

- Allergic reactions can occur with many plants, even though technically they are not poisonous. For example, 'Paper White' narcissus, orange blossom, and hyacinth all have powerful fragrances. With prolonged exposure, they may cause the nose to run, the eyes to tear, or the throat to become irritated.

- Depending on the abilities and understanding of your clients, you may wish to keep poisonous plants out of reach — in plant hangers or on high shelves — or to ban these plants from the horticulture program. If your clients are liable to ingest plants or handle them without due caution, it is best to base your program on nonhazardous plants. Table 16 provides good choices for such clients.

Hazardous and poisonous plants should be avoided until you have a good understanding of their toxicity. Once you and your

Table 16
Some of the Safe Ones

Floor Plants
Areca palm *(Chrysalidocarpus lutescens)*
Chinese rose or Chinese hibiscus *(Hibiscus rosa-sinensis)*
False aralia *(Dizygotheca elegantissima)*
Japanese aralia *(Fatsia japonica)*
Norfolk Island pine *(Araucaria heterophylla)*

Medium-height Bench
Cast-iron plant *(Aspidistra elatior)*
Jade plant *(Crassula argentea)*
Lady's palm or bamboo palm *(Rhapis excelsa)*
Polkadot plant *(Hypoestes phyllostachya)*
Sensitive plant *(Mimosa pudica)*

Small Bench
African violet *(Saintpaulia* hybrids)
Christmas cactus *(Schlumbergera bridgesii)*
Nerve plant *(Fittonia verschaffeltii)*
Radiator plant *(Peperomia verticillata)*
Staghorn fern *(Platycerium bifurcatum)*

Hangers
Button fern *(Pellaea rotundifolia)*
Grape ivy *(Cissus incisa)*
Piggyback plant *(Tolmiea menziesii)*
Spider plant *(Chlorophytum commosum 'Variegatum')*
Swedish ivy *(Plectranthus oertendahlii)*

From Baby Safe Houseplants and Cut Flowers: A Guide to Keeping Children and Plants Safely Under the Same Roof by John I. Albers and Delores M. Albers (Pownal, Vermont: Garden Way Publishing, 1993). Reprinted with permission of Storey Communications.

clients understand the risks, you can decide whether to include these plants in your program. If you decide to include them, use caution when working with them, especially if there is a risk of ingestion or contamination of the skin and eyes. Information on symptoms, toxic agent, and emergency procedures can be found in the Medical Publications section of the Resources chapter.

Table 17 lists some common hazardous or poisonous plants. It is by no means a complete list: *do not* assume that plants are safe just because they are not on this list!

Table 17. Hazardous Plants

Fields, Wooded Areas, and Swamps

Plant	Toxicity	Plant	Toxicity
Bindweed *Calystegia sepium*	Seeds have hallucinogenic effects similar to morning glory.	Nightshade *Atropa belladonna*	Berries can be fatal; affects central nervous system.
Buttercup *Ranunculus acris*	All parts — juice may severely injure digestive system.	Poison ivy and oak *Rhus radicana toxicodendron*	All parts — causes severe dermatitis.
Jack-in-the-pulpit *Arisaema triphyllum*	All parts, especially roots — causes burning of mouth and throat.	Poppy (opium) *Papaver somniferum*	Seeds — sedative effect could be dangerous if eaten in quantity.
Jimson weed *Datura stramonium*	All parts — extremely poisonous.	Virginia creeper *Parthenocissus quinquefolia*	Berries may be fatal if eaten in quantity.
May apple *Podophyllum peltatum*	Fruit has laxative effect if eaten in quantity.	Water hemlock *Cicuta maculata*	Fatal; causes painful convulsions.
Mushrooms and toadstools	All parts — should be avoided unless absolutely sure of identity.		

Ornamental Trees and Shrubs

Plant	Toxicity	Plant	Toxicity
Buckthorns *Rhamnus* spp.	Leaves and fruit are strongly cathartic (laxative).	Poplar *Populus* spp.	Female flowers create fluff that is allergenic to many.
Horse chestnut *Aesculus hippocastanum*	All parts contain dangerous glycoside, which affects the heart. Fruit may create unsure footing and hinder wheelchairs. Husks are abrasive.	Privet *Ligastrum* spp.	Berries are poisonous when ingested.
Fruit trees	Ornamental crabapples can be messy and slippery if not gathered; fruit may stain. Fermenting fruit attracts wasps, bees, etc.	Roses *Rosa* spp.	Branches have sharp spines.
Gingko tree (female) *Gingko biloba*	Fruit has a very foul odour.	Siebold viburnum *Viburnum sieboldii*	Fruit stains and has a foul odour.
English holly *Ilex aquifolium*	Berries look tempting to small children and are toxic.	Yew *Taxus* spp.	Berries (seeds) contain heart-depressing alkaloid toxins.

Outdoor Flower Gardens

Plant	Toxicity	Plant	Toxicity
Angel's trumpet *Datura metel*	All parts — a member of deadly nightshade family; has narcotic properties.	Gas plant *Dictamnus* spp.	Oily covering on stems, leaves, and seed pods may cause dermatitis.
Autumn crocus *Colchicum autumnale*	Causes vomiting and nervous excitement.	Goldenrod *Solidago virgaurea*	Pollen is an allergen.
Belladonna *Atropa belladona*	All parts (especially shiny black berries) induce hallucinations.	Iris *Iris* spp.	Rhizome causes digestive upset.
Bleed-ing heart *Dicentra spectabilis*	Foliage and roots in large amounts may be poisonous.	Larkspur *Delphinium* spp.	Young plants and seed — cause digestive upset, nervous excitement, depression; could be fatal.
Castor oil plant *Ricinus communis*	Seeds — one or two of the colorful beans could be fatal.	Lily-of-the-valley *Convallaria vajalis*	All parts — same effects as foxglove.
Comfrey *Symphytum officinale*	Roots and leaves — scientific evidence of carcinogenic (cancer-causing) properties.	Marijuana *Cannabis sativa*	Resin from female plant causes hallucinogenic effects when smoked or drunk.
Foxglove *Digitalis purpurea*	Leaves in large quantities may cause irregular heartbeat, digestive upset; may be fatal.	Monkshood *Aconitum* spp.	Fleshy roots — cause digestive upset, nervous excitement.

Outdoor Flower Gardens (cont'd)

Plant	Toxicity	Plant	Toxicity
Morning glory *Ipomoea purpurea*	Seeds have hallucinogenic effects.	Garden rhubarb *Rheum rhabarbarum*	Leaf blade — large amounts may cause convulsions, coma, death.
Petunia *Petunia* hybrids	A member of the nightshade family; all parts have hallucinogenic effects.	Star of Bethlehem *Omithogalum umbellaturn*	Vomiting and nervous excitement.
Poppy (opium) *Papaver somniferum*	Seeds — sedative effect could be dangerous if ingested in large quantities.	Tansy *Tanacetum vulgare*	Leaves and flowers have narcotic effects; large amounts may be fatal.

House Plants

Plant	Toxicity	Plant	Toxicity
Azalea *Azalea*	Can be fatal; ingestion will cause varying degrees of nausea, vomiting, depression. All parts poisonous.	Calla lily *Zantedeschia aethiopica*	Leaves and rhizome cause burning and swelling of mouth and throat, vomiting. In some cases, fragrance may be irritating.
Cacti, yucca, agave *Cacti* spp.	Spines, thorns, and barbs could cause pain and infection.	Jerusalem cherry *Solanum pseudocapsicum*	All parts cause stomach pains, paralysis, respiratory depression. Fruit looks very attractive and could be tempting if within reach.
Caladium *Caladium* hybrids	All parts cause irritation to mouth, stomach, and intestine.	Crown of thorns *Euphorbia milii*	Thorns and sap, or latex, cause skin irritation. Ingested sap causes burning and swelling in mouth.

House Plants (cont'd)

Plant	Toxicity	Plant	Toxicity
Cyclamen *Cyclamen persicum*	Ingested bulbs cause stomach cramps and diarrhea.	English ivy *Hedera helix*	Ingestion of leaves causes excitement, difficulty in breathing, coma.
Donkeytail or burro's tail *Sedum morganianum*	All parts cause vomiting and respiratory depression if swallowed. Leaf parts break off easily and may attract small children.	Lantan *Lantana* spp.	Green berries cause stomach and intestinal irritation. Volatile oil on stems and leaves could cause skin irritation.
Dumb cane *Dieffenbachia*	All parts may cause burning and irritation of mouth, swelling of tongue. May become top-heavy if not pruned back regularly.	Milk bush *Euphorbia tirucalli*	Skin and eye irritation; swelling of tongue, mouth, and throat.
Elephant ear *Colocasia* spp.	All parts may cause burning and swelling of mouth and throat.	Mistletoe *Phoradendron flavescens* and *Viscum album*	Berries fatal if ingested.
Flamingo flower *Anthurium* spp.	All parts — ingestion causes severe mouth and throat irritation.	Oleander *Nerium oleander*	Bulbs are toxic; if ingested, may cause vomiting. Hanging branches could be a physical obstacle.
Hyacinth, daffodil, tulip *Hyacinth, Narcissus, Tulipa*	Bulbs are toxic and if ingested may cause vomiting. In some cases fragrance may be irritating.	Philodendron *Philodendron* spp.	Leaves and stems — burning of mouth, vomiting, diarrhea.
Hydrangea *Hydrangea macrophylla*	Leaves and buds may cause vomiting, diarrhea.	Mother-in-law's tongue *Sansevieria trifasciata*	Leaf edge and tips very sharp.

Chapter 8

>-·◆··O··◆·i-<

Resources

Publications

There are many excellent publications available on horticulture and horticulture therapy. The publications mentioned here are those that I have found useful, but you may also want to visit your local bookstore for new books on gardening, particularly those that relate specifically to your region. This list should help you get started.

Design

Jorgensen, J. *Landscape Design for the Disabled*. McLean, VA: American Society of Landscape Architects Foundation.

This book is quite technical, dealing with specific design and construction of such things as ramps, walkups, playgrounds, and campsites for the disabled.

Newdick, Jane. *Creating Style with House-plants*. London: Octopus Books Ltd., 1985.

This is a useful reference if you are planning to try some interior landscaping in a private residence. Lots of good ideas on incorporating plants effectively. Hardcover British publication.

Equipment

Bracken, J. *Your Window Greenhouse*. New York: Thomas Y. Crowell Co., 1977.

A practical book on simple greenhouse design, plant culture, and ideas for making gardening fun.

Hobby Greenhouses in Alberta. AGDEX 731–5. Edmonton: Alberta Department of Agriculture, 1989.

A good explanation of the purpose, function, and operation of small greenhouses, along with ideas on construction.

General

Ball, Vic (ed.). *The Ball Red Book*. Chicago: Geo. J. Ball, Inc., 1980.

An excellent commercial plant production guide.

Canadian Gardening Magazine. 130 Spy Court, Markham, ON, L3R 5H6.

Commercial Storage of Fruits and Vegetables. Pub. 1532. Ottawa: Agriculture Canada.

Herwig, Rob. *How to Grow Healthy House Plants*. Tucson, AZ: HP Books, 1979.

Very useful resource manual for culture and identification of house plants. Colour prints illustrate each example.

Horticulture: The Magazine of American Gardening, P.O. Box 53879, Boulder, CO 80321.

Lloyd, G. B. *Don't Call It Dirt*. San Francisco: Bookworm Publishing Co., 1976.

An interesting little book — the light side of gardening and working in the soil.

Menage, Ronald. *Greenhouse Gardening*. Ontario: Penguin Publications, 1974.

Plants and Gardens (formerly *TLC for Plants*), Gardenvale Publishing, 1 Pacifique, Ste Anne Bellevue, PQ, H9X 1C5.

Ryotte, L. *Success with Small Food Gardens*. Charlotte, VT: Garden Way Publications, 1980.

This little paperback describes how gardening can be just as productive in a small space, and with a lot less bending and physical exertion.

University of Alberta Home Gardening Course. Edmonton: University of Alberta, 1986.

A useful reference to horticulture practices on the Prairies.

Vick, Roger. *Gardening on the Prairies*. Saskatoon: Western Producer Prairie Books, 1987.

Horticulture Therapy

Baker, Jerry. *Plants Are Like Kids*. New York: Grosset and Dunlap Publishers, 1976.

Good resource, with simple ideas on gardening with kids. Easy to read. Hardcover.

Boks, H., and P. Elliott. *The Garden and the Handicapped Child*. London: Disabled Living Foundation, 1978.

A British publication, sensitive to the application of gardening and the handicapped child, excellent drawings, full of ideas.

Burlingame, A. W. *Hoe For Health*. © 1974 Alice Wessels Burlingame.

Another one of the original texts on horticulture therapy. This book may be hard to find, but it has lots of good program ideas.

Chapin, Mary. *Gardening for the Physically Handicapped and the Elderly*. London: B. T. Batsford Ltd., 1978.

The story of how one lady makes gardening possible for her elderly mother. Easy to read. This is a British publication.

A Child's Garden. San Francisco: Chevron Chemical Co., Ortho Division, 1974.

An excellent "idea" publication. Lots of information on vegetable culture and training of vegetables. This is very useful for special education teachers.

Cotton, M. *Out of Doors with Handicapped People*. Human Horizons Series. London: Souvenir Press, 1981.

Another excellent British publication, with particular emphasis on nature study and outdoor involvement for physically handicapped people. Good drawings, with simple explanations of plants and their uses.

Dick, D. H. "Why Shouldn't Every Psychiatric Hospital Offer Horticultural Therapy?" In *Horticultural Therapy* (fact sheet). Somerset, England.

The Melwood Manual, Melwood Horticultural Training Centre, 5606 Dower House Rd., Upper Marlboro, MD 20870.

An excellent source of information on the usefulness of horticulture in working with mentally handicapped people.

Olszowy, Damon. *Horticulture for the Disabled and Disadvantaged*. Springfield, IL: Charles C. Thomas Pub., 1978.

A good overview, dealing with topics ranging from the philosophical approach to horticulture therapy to practical activities that benefit the disabled and disadvantaged. The benefits of blending horticulture with other activities in health care settings are made clear.

Please, Peter A. *Children's Gardening*. Frome, Somerset, England: Horticulture Therapy, 1991, 1993.

A month by month guide to advancing educational gardening activities in schools.

Thoday, P. R. "Therapy Through Horticulture." In *British Association for the Advancement of Science, Annual Meeting*. University of Bath, UK: 1978.

Thoday, P. R., and M. J. Sargent. *Hospital Grounds Utilization*. University of Bath, UK: 1974.

White, A. S. *Easy Path to Gardening*. London: Reader's Digest Association, 1972.

One of the original publications specific to this subject. Lots of excellent illustrations and ideas for modifying gardens and gardening.

Medical

Clayman, Charles B. *The American Medical Association Encyclopedia of Medicine*. New York: Random House, 1989.

Kadans, Joseph. *Encyclopedia of Medicinal Herbs*. New York: ARCO Pub., 1970.

Schultes, Richard. *Hallucinogenic Plants*. New York: Golden Press, 1976.

Pests

Back Yard Pest Management. AGDEX 605–2. Edmonton: Alberta Department of Agriculture, 1990.

A newspaper-like fact sheet on pests and diseases common to prairie gardens and house plants.

"Insect and Disease Control in the Home Garden." Pub. 64. Toronto: Ontario Ministry of Agriculture and Food.

Ives, W. G. H., and H. R. Wong. *Tree and Shrub Insects of the Prairie Provinces*. Canadian Forestry Service, 1988.

Mengersen, Ernest W., and Hugh Phillip. *Insect Pests on the Prairies*. Edmonton: University of Alberta, 1988.

Colour prints illustrate the common insect pests found in natural and urban areas of the Prairies.

Plants

Buckley, A. R. *Canadian Garden Perennials*. Saanichton, BC: Hancock House, 1977.

A comprehensive guide to hardy perennials for Canada; includes a hardiness zone map. Some colour prints.

Canada Department of Forestry. *Native Trees of Canada*. Ottawa: Queen's Printer, 1968.

Herwig, Rob. *The Edible Garden*. Twickenham, UK: Hamlyn Publishers, 1986.

This hardcover book describes vegetable and fruit gardening. Lovely colour prints, with each vegetable, small fruit, and herb described separately.

Knowles, Hugh. *Woody Ornamentals for the Prairies*. Edmonton: University of Alberta, 1989.

Complete reference guide to woody plants, trees, and shrubs, with colour prints.

Peterson, Lee. *A Field Guide to Edible Wild Plants*. Boston: Houghton Mifflin Co., 1977.

A complete guide to edible wild plants of North America, along with some that are poisonous.

Shewchuk, George W. *Rose Gardening on the Prairies*. Edmonton: University of Alberta, 1988.

Taylor, Norman. *The Guide to Garden Shrubs and Trees*. Boston: Houghton Mifflin Co., 1965.

A comprehensive guide to the identification and culture of garden trees and shrubs of North America.

Toop, Edgar W. *Annuals for the Prairies*. Edmonton: University of Alberta, Saskatoon: University of Saskatchewan, and Edmonton: Lone Pine Press, 1993.

Excellent publication describing annuals useful to Prairie gardens.

Toop, Edgar W., and Sara Williams. *Perennials for the Prairies*. Edmonton: University of Alberta, and Saskatoon: University of Saskatchewan, 1991.

An excellent publication, with colour prints and complete descriptions of perennials for the Canadian Prairies and Northern Plains.

Films and Slide Presentations

Christenson, Thomas A. *My Garden*. Baltimore: Mass Media Ministries.

A colour video presenting a beautiful photographic message of faith and hope.

Everyone's Business. 1982.

A colour video about a co-operative greenhouse venture owned by a disabled group in Saskatoon, Saskatchewan.

Friends: A Junior/Senior Program. Canadian Film Board.

A video showing a co-operative program between school children and seniors at the Extended Care Unit of the University of British Columbia.

Growing Together. Canadian Film Board.

A slide-tape presentation a family program at the Extended Care Unit of the University of British Columbia.

Ruth Stout's Garden. American Council of Therapy and Rehabilitation Through Horticulture.

This video provides a wonderful depiction of one woman's determination.

The Vacant Lot. Canadian Film Board, 1977.

A colour video about an inspiring community seniors' garden in Montreal.

Horticulture Therapy Training Programs

United States

Edmonds Community College
Lynwood, WA 98036
(206) 640–1604

Kansas State University
Department of Horticulture
Manhattan, KS 66502
(913) 532–6011

Herbert H. Lehman College
The City University of New York
Bronx, NY 10468
(718) 960–8000

Texas A & M University
Department of Horticulture
College Station, TX 77840
(409) 845–5341

Virginia State University
Blacksburg, VA 24061
(703) 231–6000

Canada

    Homewood Health Centre
    150 Delhi Street
    Guelph, ON, N1E 6K9
    (519) 824–1010

United Kingdom

    Mary Marlborough Lodge
    Nuffield Orthopaedic Centre
    Headington, Oxford, UK
    OX3 7LD

United Kingdom

    Horticultural Therapy
    Goulds Ground, Vallis Way
    Frome, Somerset
    UK BA113DW

United States

    American Council for Therapy and
    Rehabilitation Through Horticulture
    9220 Wightman Road, Suite 300
    Gaithersburg, MD 20879

Seminars and Courses

Holden Arboretum
Mentor, OH 44060

Chicago Botanic Garden
Glencoe, IL 60022

Clemson University
Clemson, SC 29634

Melwood Horticultural Training Center
5606 Dower House Road
Upper Marlboro, MD 20870

Associations

Canada

    Canadian Horticulture Therapy Association
    c/o Royal Botanical Garden
    P.O. Box 399
    Hamilton, ON, L8N 3H8

Equipment

In addition to discussing your needs with local firms, you may wish to consider obtaining catalogues from the following suppliers.

Canada

    Dominion Seed House
    115 Guelph St.
    Georgetown, ON, L7G 4A2
    Mail-order seed house; also carry a limited number of tools.

    Floralight Gardens Canada Inc.
    P.O. Box 247, Station A
    Willowdale, ON, M2N 5S9
    Artificial-light gardens.

    Forester W. E. I.
    Box 788
    Calgary, AB, T2P 2J8
    Tools.

Gardeners Supply Co. Ltd.
949 Wilson Ave.
Downsview, ON, M3K 1G2
Tools.

Lee Valley Tools
P.O. Box 6295, Station J
Ottawa, ON, K2A 1T4
An excellent supplier of anatomically correct and modified tools for handicapped gardeners.

Marpost Industries Ltd.
159 Bay St.
Suite 2.4
Toronto, ON, M5J 1J7
Tools and materials for artificial-light gardens.

Ontario Turf Equipment Ltd.
540 Charles Side Rd.
London, ON, N5V 2C7
Large supplier of mowers, wheelbarrows, electrical and mechanical tools.

Westcan Horticultural Supplies
Bay 5, 6112 30th St. S. E.

Calgary, AB
Lightweight pots, jiffy-7's, cell packs, etc.

United States

Denmon & Co.
2913 Saturn St., Suite G
Brea, CA 92621
Horticultural equipment.

Gothic Area Greenhouses
Dept. H-14
P.O. Box 1564
Mobile, AL, 36601
Greenhouses.

Tube Craft Inc.
134Z W. 80 St.
Cleveland, OH 44102
Fluorescent-light gardens.

Vermont-Ware
Dept. 1801
Ainesburg, VT 05461
Garden carts.

Glossary

Action plant   A plant that exhibits some sort of visible movement in response to movement, darkness, or touching.

Air layering   Roots forming on the aerial part of the plant where the stem has been girdled or slit at an upward angle.

Algicide   A type of herbicide designed to control algae.

Anatomically correct   Designed to fit a particular body part (e.g., the hand).

Atrium   An indoor courtyard of plants.

Botrytis   A common mould or fungal infection.

Canes   The branches producing fruit on raspberry and blackberry bushes.

Client   A person for whom professional services are rendered.

Damping-off   A common fungal disease, especially in seedlings.

Deadheading   Removing spent or faded flowers, thus preventing seeding and encouraging continued flowering.

Deciduous   Plants that lose their leaves during the winter months.

Dibbler   A small dowel, rounded at one end, used to make a hole to insert seedling.

Direct sowing   Sowing seed into prepared outdoor seed bed.

Disability   Temporary loss or permanent impairment of a body function (e.g., loss of sight).

Espalier   A method of training plants such as dwarf fruit trees to grow along wire.

Everlastings   Plants with flowers and stems

that retain most of their fresh form or colour when air dried.

Forcing   Bringing dormant tree or shrub branches into bloom quickly, using warmth and darkness; causing hardy bulbs such as tulips to bloom indoors by first giving them a 12 to 14 week "cold" period.

Germination test   A test to determine the percentage of viable seed in packet, usually carried out on seeds that are more than a year old.

Handicap   A disadvantage for a given individual, resulting from an impairment or disability, that limits or prevents the fulfilment of a role that is considered as normal, depending on age, sex, and social and cultural factors, for that individual.

Hard landscaping   Materials such as tiles, rocks, or stones used as retaining walls or walkways in the landscape.

Hardening   The process of acclimatizing plants, usually from an indoor environment to outdoor conditions.

Hot caps   Plastic or paper coverings used to cover tender transplants.

Impairment   Any loss or abnormality of psychological, physiological, or anatomical structure or function.

Master Gardener program   A program that trains lay persons to do voluntary service in horticulture.

Oasis   A foam-like, moisture-absorbent medium used to support flowers and foliage in flower arrangements.

Patient   A person receiving care within an institution.

Pesticide   Any material used to control insects, diseases, or weeds.

Reality orientation   A set of activities or attitudes used by health care workers to help keep a resident in touch with present day living.

Recreation   The activities a person becomes involved in for fun or relaxation.

Response   A noticed change in behaviour elicited by internal or external stimuli.

Rhizome   A horizontal underground stem that forms both roots and shoots at nodes.

Secateurs   A garden tool used to prune shrubs, trees, and flowers.

Selective response   The process of evaluating a situation to make a decision (e.g., deciding which plants need to be watered).

Stock plants   Parent (usually one- to two-year-old) plants from which cuttings are made.

Succession cropping   Planting a second crop

soon after or just before the first has
been harvested.

True leaves   Usually, the first set of leaves
after the primary or "seed" leaves have
developed on seedlings.

The Author

Lynn Dennis received his Diploma in Horticulture from the Niagara Parks Commission, School of Horticulture, Niagara Falls, Ontario, in 1969. He holds a Certificate in Child Development and Learning from McMaster University and a Certificate as a Personal Care Aide from the Alberta Vocational College. He has over twenty years' experience using horticulture as a therapeutic medium, and is currently working as a caregiver and horticultural consultant to the Canterbury Foundation in Edmonton.

Lynn Dennis is a charter member of the American Council for Rehabilitation and Therapy through Horticulture, and was co-founder of the Horticulture and Therapy Association (Hamilton-Guelph region) in the early 1970s. He has conducted many work-shops on horticulture therapy for health-care professionals throughout Canada.